Tudor Princes and Princesses

Tudor Princes and Princesses

The Early Lives of the Children of Henry VII and Elizabeth of York

Aimee Fleming

First published in Great Britain in 2025 by
Pen and Sword History
An imprint of
Pen & Sword Books Ltd
Yorkshire - Philadelphia

ISBN: 978 1 39903 411 1

A CIP catalogue record for this book is available from the British Library

Typeset in INDIA by IMPEC eSolutions
Printed and bound in the England by CPI Group (UK) Ltd, Croydon, CRO 4YY

The Publisher's authorised representative in the EU for product safety is Authorised Rep Compliance Ltd., Ground Floor, 71 Lower Baggot Street, Dublin D02 P593, Ireland.
www.arccompliance.com

For a complete list of Pen & Sword titles please contact:

PEN & SWORD BOOKS LTD
47 Church Street, Barnsley, South Yorkshire, S70 2AS, UK.
E-mail: enquiries@pen-and-sword.co.uk
Website: www.pen-and-sword.co.uk

or

PEN AND SWORD BOOKS,
1950 Lawrence Road, Havertown, PA 19083, USA
E-mail: Uspen-and-sword@casematepublishers.com
Website: www.penandswordbooks.com

Contents

Acknowledgements

It is always hard to know where to begin when saying thank you. I have so many people to include, who have helped, supported – and just straight put up with me over the course of writing this book.

Firstly and the most important, thank you so much to my husband Drew, and my three wonderful boys. You have helped me, brought me tea and done everything I have asked for and more. I am truly grateful and I was only able to get here because of you.

A big thank you to the staff at Pen and Sword too, and I will always be grateful for the opportunities you have given me. To my editor, Karyn Burnham, thank you for your patience and guidance. I genuinely would not have been able to get to the end of this without your help. To my fellow historians, who have helped with sources, images, answering all sort of questions, and reassuring me when it all got too much, the biggest of big thanks!

Introduction

On 7 August 1485, a fleet of ships carrying an invading army, made up of men from all over Europe, landed at Mill Bay in Pembrokeshire. Upon their arrival, a young man disembarked and stepped onto the sand, speaking out loud the words of Psalm 43 which is traditionally the prayer said in times of trouble. He prayed to God, 'Judge me, O Lord, and favour my cause', strode up the beach and looked out on a land that he had left some fourteen years earlier as a teenager.[1] In all honesty, he probably believed he would never see it again.

The man on the beach was Henry Tudor, the Earl of Richmond, heir to the house of Lancaster and claimant of the throne of England. He had spent years in exile, travelling secretly between friendly towns and ports in Brittany and France, but had now returned with an army of soldiers and mercenaries supportive of his cause: his claim to be king of England.

On the throne then was Richard III, brother to the deceased King Edward IV, the Yorkist king who had ruled for over a decade before his untimely death in 1483 at the relatively young age of 40. Richard had then risen to the throne following the disappearance of his brother's sons, the 12-year-old King Edward V and his 9-year-old brother, Richard, Duke of York. Two short years from Edward IV's death, Richard's reign was cast into a shadow of doubt with the arrival of the young Welshman.

As Henry's retinue marched across England, gaining support, men and backing as they went, Richard mustered an army to meet him with equal force. The two sides finally faced one another at Market Bosworth, Leicestershire, on 22 August 1485, at what would come to be known as the Battle of Bosworth. The battle was fierce and fought with 'great severity' according to chroniclers writing after the event.[2]

According to Polydore Vergil, royal historian to Henry VII, Richard III fought his way through Henry's personal bodyguard and 'was killed fighting manfully in the press of his enemies'.[3] On that day, when Richard was killed, Henry emerged victorious as King Henry VII of England. The crown was, according to sources writing about the battle, knocked from Richard's head prior to his death and then, having been found 'amonge the spoile in the fielde', was brought back to Henry's camp and placed upon his head to shouts of 'God Save King Henry' from his supporters.[4] Thus, Henry became the last English monarch to be declared king through such violent means.

The events of Bosworth were the culmination of decades of conflict between the two families, the houses of Lancaster and York, in what is sometimes called 'the Cousins' War' but would come to be called the Wars of the Roses. Through the many battles, conflicts and executions of different family members for misdemeanours, the two houses were gradually left with fewer and fewer true claimants to the throne. By the time Richard III took the throne in 1483, there was just a handful of individuals who could have claimed the crown, and only Henry Tudor remained on the Lancaster line.[5]

Henry Tudor was descended from two different lines both of which could, in different ways, claim the throne of England. His father was the half-brother of King Henry VI, through their mother Catherine de Valois. She married the Welshman Owen Tudor following the death of Henry V in 1422. Her son Henry succeeded his father when he was just an infant, and she went on to have three sons with Owen, the eldest being Edmund, who became the 1st Earl of Richmond. In 1455 Edmund married Margaret Beaufort, the only daughter of John Beaufort, the Duke of Somerset and a descendent of John of Gaunt. Margaret was only 9 years old when her father died and she was placed in the wardship of Edmund, who was entrusted with her care. She was previously betrothed to John de la Pole, but this match was annulled in 1453, and Edmund decided to marry her himself. She was just 12 when the marriage took place, and when Edmund died suddenly in late 1456, Margaret was 13, a widow and pregnant with their child.[6] Margaret was taken in by her brother-in-law, Jasper Tudor, who was by this time the Earl of Pembroke, and she gave birth to her son, Henry, at Pembroke Castle in January 1457.

When Henry was born, his claim to the throne was slight. He was not considered a serious contender until much later when, in 1470 and 1471, the throne was passed to and from the Lancastrian Henry VI and the Yorkist Edward IV. The return of the throne to Edward in 1471 and then the death of Henry VI's son, Edward of Westminster, at the Battle of Tewkesbury on 4 May, meant that the 14-year-old Henry Tudor, along with the handful of other equally obscure Lancastrian claimants, were all that remained of the opposition to Edward IV's rule. Henry was taken into exile by his Uncle Jasper and they remained there until the events of 1483 meant there was enough support for Henry to make his claim. In 1485 he gathered his troops, made his bid for the throne and claimed victory.

However, as decisive as his victory may have been, Henry VII still had a lot of work to do. He had taken the throne by force, but now he needed to keep hold of it, bolster his position and ensure he was able to establish himself unquestionably as monarch. He chose to do this in a number of ways, the first he had set in motion before he even setting foot on that beach in Wales, and that was to make a marriage which would secure both his claim, and that of his future heirs. His chosen spouse was Elizabeth of York.

Elizabeth of York was the eldest daughter of Edward IV and his wife, Elizabeth Woodville. She was 17 years old when her father died, her brothers – the so-called 'Princes in the Tower' – had disappeared, and her uncle had taken over the throne as Richard III.[7] She was the most senior royal woman after the queen and was originally betrothed to the king of France, Charles VIII. This arrangement had fallen apart in 1483 when, in order to claim the throne for himself, Richard III declared the marriage between Edward IV and Elizabeth Woodville to be illegitimate and therefore all of the children were too. Their claims to the throne were null and void, and their positions at court were stripped. However, the princess and others who remained loyal to Edward IV and his offspring still believed their claim to be valid, and so Elizabeth became a precious commodity in the competition for the throne of England.

Henry had begun negotiations and declared his intentions to marry Elizabeth as early as 1483, when he attended services at Rennes cathedral on Christmas Day and in a ceremony 'undertook to marry Elizabeth of York [...] when opportunity allowed, [and] those present took an oath to him as if he were already King'.[8] He saw that their marriage would be beneficial to his cause, legitimise his claim through marriage to Edward IV's daughter and hopefully inspire loyalty in former Yorkist supporters, and this would hopefully ensure stability of the nation as a whole.

In fact, this had also been apparent to her uncle, Richard III. In the Croyland Chronicle, the author writes:

> it is said by many that the King was bent either on the anticipated death of the Queen taking place, or else by means of a divorce ... on contracting a marriage with the said Elizabeth. For it appeared that in no other way could his kingly power be established or the hopes of his rival being put to an end.[9]

Richard, her own uncle, could see how beneficial a marriage to Elizabeth would be, especially in securing his own claim. However, their close relationship did raise eyebrows at court when his intentions and attentions became clear. According to the Croyland Chronicles, even his most trusted advisors were counselling him against a marriage with Elizabeth, suggesting people would think he was doing it to 'gratify an incestuous passion for his neice'.[10]

Even though they were not so closely related as Richard and Elizabeth were, Henry had to request papal dispensation for their marriage to take place. This was due to their close 'consanguinity', or family and genetic ties. They shared some common ancestors, namely both Henry and Elizabeth had lineage back to Edward III, and so for them to marry, permission had to be granted by the Pope.[11] The couple did not wait for the Pope's approval however, approaching instead his representative, the papal legate Giacomo Passarelli, the Bishop of Imola. The document read:

> the said King Henry has, by God's providence won his realm of England, and is in peaceful possession thereof [...] desires to take the said lady to wife, but cannot do so without dispensation, inasmuch as they are related in the fourth and fourth degrees of kindred, wherefore petition is make on their behalf to the said legate to grant them dispensation by his apostolic authority to contract marriage and remain therein, notwithstanding the said impediment of kindred, and to decree the offspring to be born thereof legitimate.[12]

The last line in this petition is of particular importance. After the events of 1483 had seen Elizabeth and her siblings declared illegitimate, both Henry and Elizabeth would have wanted there to be no doubt in anyone's mind that any heirs born to them would be legitimate and with that, there would be less chance of any challenges from other claimants that may wish to challenge for the throne.

Of equal importance to Henry and to Elizabeth was ensuring that much of the country, at all levels, supported Henry as king. Henry knew that having Elizabeth as queen would help to bolster this support, especially among those who formerly supported the Yorkist monarchy. While it was crucial to Henry that he be seen as king in his own right, it was also a priority to cement the union of the two families and follow through on his promise to marry the princess.

On 10 December 1485, Henry VII stood before parliament and they in turn requested that he:

> take for himself as wife and consort the noble Lady Elizabeth, daughter of King Edward the Fourth, form which marriage, by the grace of God, it is hoped by many that there would arise offspring of the race of kings for the comfort of the whole realm.[13]

Henry replied that 'it would give him pleasure to do so', and that 'it would give him pleasure to comply with their request'. The date for the wedding was set for the following January, and immediately following this decision the wheels were set in motion to make all arrangements as swiftly as possible. Elizabeth was declared to be the Duchess of York, as 'heiress to her father and her other illustrious forebears', again to try to sway the Yorkist factions still at court that the union was in everyone's best interest.[14]

Henry was not the only one working towards this marriage though, as other interested parties were involved behind the scenes ensuring that the union went ahead. Henry's mother, Margaret Beaufort, and Elizabeth's mother, Elizabeth Woodville, were both interested in seeing the best match possible for their children. According to Thomas Penn in his book *The Winter King*, the two women negotiated in secret in the period leading up to Henry's invasion. They used priests and astrologers to act as go-betweens and carry communications between them, even getting through the guarded gates of Westminster where Elizabeth Woodville and her children were housed at the time.[15] For former Queen Elizabeth, it is easy to see that a match for her daughter with Henry Tudor was much more appealing than marrying her uncle and possibly causing problems for them all further down the line. However, any marriage promised to bring her children out of obscurity and lift the claims of illegitimacy that Richard had levelled at them.

Elizabeth herself may also have had an opinion on a potential marriage. Writing during the reign of Henry VII on the subject of her potential marriage to her uncle, Polydore Vergil says that 'the young lady herself and all others, did abhor this wickedness so detestable. To such a marriage the girl had a singular aversion.'[16]

As a woman of 19 when Henry invaded, she would have been well aware of the future of England being in the balance.

While she would not have had any influence in the matter, she and the rest of her family would have been watching with bated breath to see the outcome of the battle at Bosworth.

When Henry defeated Richard III at Bosworth, however, his first priority was to cement his own position as king of England. He had not been expected to win the battle; although it had always been his intention, his claim was not seen as strong and his forces were outnumbered by those of Richard. On the day itself, interventions on the parts of his supporters such as the Stanleys, along with some luck and Richard's death in the fighting itself, all led to his unexpected victory. Following Henry's victory, it was incredibly important that he be seen as the rightful king, and so after his triumphant arrival in London and his initial celebrations, his coronation was swiftly arranged for 30 October 1485.

We do have some information about what happened on the day itself. Bernard André, Henry's court historian, describes the event as a 'most excellent coronation' and other sources give us some indication of just what those lucky enough to attend would have experienced.[17] The chronicler Edward Hall writes that:

> he with great pompe was conveighed to Westmynster, and there the thyrtye day of Octobre was with all cerymones accustomed, enoyted & crouned kyng by the whole assent as well of the commons as of the nobilitie, & was named kyng Henry the vii of that name [...] Which kyndome he obtained & enjoyed as a thing by

> God elected & provided, and by his especiall favoure and gracious aspect compassed and acheved.[18]

He then goes on to list the royals who attended, including Charles VIII of France and James III of Scotland; their presence indicates that Henry was accepted as king by the other ruling houses and this would have been a boon to his campaign.[19] The ceremony itself would have been a spectacle, just as coronations of English monarchs always are, but Henry spared no expense to make the best impression that he could, and to inspire the confidence of his subjects. Henry's coronation was designed solely to impress, in the hope that it would stop any negativity towards his rule. Historian Roger Lockyer notes how, throughout his reign, Henry 'deliberately cultivated pomp and ceremony in order to raise the throne above the reach of even the greatest noble'.[20]

Following Henry's coronation, and having cemented his position as monarch in his own right, attention was then allowed to turn to the royal wedding, and the joining of the houses of Lancaster and York. In joining the two, Henry and Elizabeth could pave the way for a peaceful England, and again this would be done through ceremony and a great deal of pomp and pageantry. Hall again writes about the marriage through which he says that the 'old divided controversy' would be 'buried and perpetually extinct' by the union of Henry and Elizabeth.[21]

> yet there lacked a wrest to the harpeto set all the strynges in a monacordeand tune which was the matrimony to be fineshed betwene the kynge and the lady Elizabeth

> daughter to kyng Edward, which lyke a good prynce according to his othe and promes, he did both solemnise and cosummate in brief tyme after, that is to saye on the the xviij. daye of January. By reason of whiche manage peace was thought to discende outc of heaue into England, consideryng that the lynes of Lancastre & Yorke, being both noble families equiualet in ryches, fame and honour, were now brought into one knot and connexed together, of whose two bodyes one heyre might succede, which after their lyme should peaceably rule and enioye the whole monarchy and realme of England.[22]

This description would inspire Shakespeare to write about the union:

> we will unite the white rose and the red;
> Smile heaven, upon this fair conjunction,
> That hath frowned upon their enmity![23]

When the wedding took place in January 1486, it was again an extravagant affair. Crowds lined the route, even in the middle of winter, to see the couple, and delegates came from all over Europe. It was a key event and marked a symbolic end to a decades-long conflict during which England had lost position, money, and a generation of young nobles and fighting-age men.

Huge banners of Welsh dragons and other symbols of the new house of 'Tudor' were strewn all over the abbey where the ceremony took place. Their marriage formed the house of Tudor, the linking of the two houses of Lancaster and York both physically through their marriage, but also symbolically through the newly designed 'Tudor Rose', showing the red and white roses merged together, which festooned everything that was produced for the couple.

The ultimate symbol of their unity, however, would to be the production of an heir, and very soon after their marriage, Elizabeth was pregnant. She gave birth to a boy in late 1486; a son and heir for the new Tudor dynasty, and the physical amalgamation of the two houses. This would surely bring peace and harmony to the kingdom. It was a blessing and proof that Henry's victory over Richard III's forces and his claiming the throne had been God's will, and proof also that Henry really was, as he had claimed to be, 'divinely ordained to quell political turbulence by marrying the daughter of Edward IV'.[24]

Despite all of these good omens, not everyone was happy or supportive of the new regime. Many Yorkists were still unhappy about Henry's rule and no amount of showmanship, or even the 'conciliatory gesture of marring Edward IVs daughter' would change their minds.[25] Some were plotting behind the scenes to have one of their own claimants challenge Henry, take the throne and then to rule in his stead.

As early as 1487, just two years after he had won the Battle of Bosworth, Henry faced a new Yorkist force at the Battle of Stoke, and this time they were led by a young boy who claimed to be the rightful king of England. The Battle of Stoke is considered to be the last battle of the Wars of the Roses;

Henry won and the 'boy king' was exposed as a pretender by the name of Lambert Simnel. Henry set to work bolstering and rebuilding his position on the throne – he even pardoned Simnel and gave him a job as a turnspit in the royal kitchens, proving that he was indeed neither claimant to the throne nor rival to Henry.

Henry also sought to settle unrest by, finally, arranging a coronation for Elizabeth – almost two years after their marriage and a year after the birth of their son. While Henry's victory at Stoke had been decisive, and his actions immediately following the uprising had seen some of his major opposition dealt with through attainders, seizures of land – and even, in some cases, imprisonment and execution – the situation was still precarious. By installing Edward IV's daughter as official queen consort, it could be construed that Henry and Elizabeth wanted to draw a line under the whole affair and concentrate on ruling as a pair, raising their children, providing an heir and a secure future for their family – and therefore the entire country.

It was crucial that Henry and Elizabeth presented a united front; at her coronation Elizabeth was very much presented a 'Tudor Queen' rather than 'Yorkist Princess'. Heraldic symbols such as Welsh dragons and Tudor roses appeared all over for the ceremony, and her role as mother to Prince Arthur, the heir to this new dynasty, was highlighted throughout. She, as the wife and consort of the king, had the potential to lay the foundations for the success of England, through the provision of more legitimate and incontrovertible heirs to the throne.

It is clear that their children were central to the success of the reigns of Henry VII and Elizabeth of York. Although their marriage had brought the two houses together ceremonially, their children united the houses both physically and symbolically.

Henry and Elizabeth had both had unstable childhoods, and violent and sometimes traumatic ascents to the throne – and now they had an uncertain future. Their situation, both as parents and monarchs, led them to make decisions and hold attitudes towards their children that would have a lasting impact on the children, and on the story of England and of Europe in the Tudor period and beyond.

Chapter 1

Before the House of Tudor

The childhoods of both Henry and Elizabeth were intrinsically very different from one another. This may well have caused issues as they became parents themselves and had to raise their offspring, on whom the hopes of this new dynasty and future for England were pinned.

Henry had a very unusual childhood, even for the fifteenth century. He was an only child, born to a widowed mother, Margaret Beaufort, who was herself only a child at the time. She gave birth to her only son just a few short months after turning 13 years old, raising him alone following the death of his father, Edmund Tudor, while he was being held prisoner. He most likely died of a plague or sickness that was reported to have swept through southern Wales.[1]

Henry was born in January 1457 at Pembroke Castle. Initially his childhood appeared to be fairly normal – or as close to normal as possible in a time of civil war and conflict that involved close members of his family. Following his father's death, the responsibility for his care was taken up by his uncle, Jasper Tudor, and he was given an education and upbringing befitting his station. He did enjoy some comforts and status given by virtue of his uncle being the stepbrother to the king,

Henry VI, but nothing much was really expected of a boy who was distantly related to the royal house.

However, this position within the royal family changed considerably in 1461 when Henry VI was deposed by Edward, Earl of March, newly crowned as the Yorkist Edward IV. Henry VI and his Lancastrian supporter family were pushed aside in favour of the Yorkists, and as such the Tudor family were pushed back, and Jasper Tudor went into exile. Henry was put into the care of William Herbert, who was given Jasper's title as Earl of Pembroke, and also his home at Pembroke Castle. Herbert was also given Henry's wardship and as part of that he ensured that the young boy received a good education at Pembroke and at his other home at Raglan Castle.[2] While very few records survive about this period of Henry's life, it is likely that his childhood looked much like most other boys of his station and background. He had a tutor, Andreas Scotus, who would have been responsible for his education; he would have been taught to play musical instruments, read and write in English and Latin, and to speak French and possibly Welsh.[3] It is likely that Henry's nurses and other carers came from the local area, and while his tuition in the Welsh language may not have been as formal as the rest of his education, he certainly seems to have been familiar with Welsh history, myths, legends and language later in life. He also would have been taught more knightly skills, to fight and to joust, to dance and have courtly manners ready for when he was able to join the rest of the court in London.[4]

Henry was most likely separated from his mother for prolonged periods. She had married Sir Henry Stafford in

1458 and while she would have seen her son on occasion, it was not unusual in this period for noble children to be separated from their parents for long periods of time. However, Henry would be her only child, and as she had him in such traumatic circumstances it can be imagined that the young mother found it very difficult to part with her child, even if he was in the care of such a kind benefactor.

The situation changed abruptly in October 1470 however, when the Earl of Warwick rose up against Edward IV, freed Henry VI from the Tower, and restored him to the throne. This re-elevation of the Lancastrian family allowed some of the family members, like the Tudors, to reacquaint themselves with court life, and show just what they were able to do. Jasper Tudor wasted no time returning to England and in bringing his young nephew to court, where he introduced the boy, now 12 years old, to his stepbrother, the king.

Henry VI was supposedly impressed with the youngster, and said: 'This is he unto whom both we and our adversaries must yield and give over the dominion.'[5]

Henry VI's restoration was a short one however. His Lancastrian forces were defeated first at the Battle of Barnet on 14 April, and then finally, on 4 May 1471 at the Battle of Tewkesbury. Henry's only son and heir, Edward of Westminster, was killed at Tewkesbury, and the Earl of Warwick died at Barnet. Henry was captured when Edward IV entered London on 21 May, and he died shortly after in the Tower of London. These events, the deaths of so many in the battles at Barnet and Tewkesbury, and then the death of Henry VI, made the young

Henry Tudor one of only a handful of claimants to the throne on the Lancastrian side of the family. This inevitably put him in danger, his life threatened by those who would eliminate him from the list of claimants. Sensing this imminent risk his uncle Jasper took the boy, now 14 years old, into exile in Brittany. Henry left behind everything he had ever known, including his mother. Margaret's husband, Sir Henry Stafford, had been badly wounded at the Battle of Barnet and would never recover from his wounds. She remained with her husband to nurse him and would not see her son until his return from the Continent fourteen years later.

While in exile, Henry was joined by other loyal Lancastrian supporters. Alongside his uncle, there was also the Earl of Oxford and a contingent of others who supported the Lancastrian cause and were exiled from England as a result. They travelled from town to town and were sent support and news from those closest to him who remained in England. During his reign Edward IV even sent gold and other gifts to Francis II, Duke of Brittany, in return for him sending Henry Tudor back to England, promising that it was for the purposes of a marriage to ally him with the Yorkist royal family. Henry's mother Margaret sensed that it was a deception and cautioned him not to take up the offer, and Duke Francis, instead of handing Henry over, offered him sanctuary in St Malo.[6]

Things changed overnight in 1483 when King Edward IV died unexpectedly at the young age of 40; Henry became the focus of the Lancastrian claim to the English throne.

Edward had left a young son and heir, Edward V, who was only 12 years old. When he succeeded it was intended that his uncle, Richard of Gloucester, would stand in as protector and advise the young king. However, within a few weeks of his succession, Richard had claimed that his brother's marriage to Elizabeth Woodville had been invalid because Edward was already married to Eleanor Talbot, Lady Butler, when their wedding had taken place. As a result, Richard claimed, all of Edward and Elizabeth's children, including the young King Edward V, were illegitimate, and could not make a valid claim to the throne. Richard therefore claimed that he was the rightful heir, taking to the throne as King Richard III.

Richard's actions were seen, even by some loyal Yorkists, as a usurpation of the throne. Support began to rally around other claimants to the English crown, and at the top of that list of claimants was Henry Tudor. He was visited by nobles in exile, sent money, and many pledged their allegiance to him while he was still in exile. He even gained the backing of the nobility in Brittany and of the French king.

In 1483 a group of nobles led by the Duke of Buckingham, and heavily influenced by Henry's mother, Margaret Beaufort, attempted to stage a coup to drive Richard III off the throne and replace him with Henry. While this rebellion failed, it shows the strength of support that Henry had among Richard's dissenters, and so, in 1485, a little over two years after Richard claimed the throne for himself, Henry and his forces set out to take England in the name of Lancaster, and in the name of Tudor.

So, we can see that Henry Tudor's upbringing and childhood, particularly his teen years, could not be described as settled. Indeed, he himself acknowledged just how unusual his childhood had been, as Commines, a writer and chronicler who was present at the Burgundian court while Henry was in exile there, recalls in a conversation when the king said that 'from the age of five years old he had been either a fugitive or a captive'.[7] But, while Henry had his childhood in Wales, and then in exile in Europe, his future bride Elizabeth was experiencing a very different, but equally unsettled, upbringing.

Elizabeth was born in January 1466. She was the first-born child to Edward IV and his wife and queen Elizabeth Woodville, who would go on to have ten children altogether. Her arrival was much anticipated; a male heir would secure Edward IV on the throne and would put down any dissenters who disagreed with his marriage to Elizabeth Woodville, or his claim to the throne of England. If this sounds familiar, it is because this is practically the same situation that the Princess Elizabeth would find herself in with her husband, Henry VII. Only this time, the queen gave birth to a girl, a princess – the first princess to be born to a king of England in a century. Despite the disappointment and anguish regarding her gender, the arrival of a healthy baby was still a cause for celebration and the king and queen still put on an extravagant ceremonial baptism in St Stephen's Chapel at Westminster. They also made a major event out of the queen's churching ceremony which followed a number of weeks after Elizabeth's birth, in an attempt to secure further the king and queen's position and make sure that all of them, including any further children, were fully recognised and respected.[8]

Elizabeth spent her early years in her nursery, in the care of wet-nurses and her lady governess, Lady Margaret Berners. She would have been swaddled tightly to ensure that her limbs grew straight and, as an infant princess, there were even servants employed solely to rock the cradle while she slept and to watch over her in the night.[9] Everything she required would have been provided, and this luxury would have been apparent to the little princess from a very young age. Her father, the king, ran a luxurious, opulent court, which was described by one admirer as 'the most splendid court that could be found in all Christendom.'[10] The households of the king and the queen comprised hundreds of people, grand palaces that they would move between, luxurious clothing and extravagant food.

In August 1467 the Princess Mary was born, this time at Windsor Castle. In this same year the queen was granted Sheen Palace as part of her estates for life and it would appear that its purpose was as a nursery for the young royal children. It was probably deemed suitable for this purpose due to its location outside of the city of London, 'because the air … being somewhat at large, the place is healthy; and the noise not so much, and so consequently quiet'.[11] The household of the young princesses, led by Lady Berners, spent a lot of time at Sheen, but it did move around to other palaces similarly situated around London, notably Eltham Palace in Kent. In 1469 another princess, Cecily, joined the nursery, and the children, up to that point had had a stable and typical royal experience.

However, in 1470 when Henry VI retook the throne, the situation became tumultuous. Elizabeth's father, Edward IV, was forced into exile, running away from his throne as he was defeated by the forces of the Earl of Warwick and Queen Margaret, wife of Henry VI. Edward's queen, Elizabeth Woodville, could not go into exile however. She had young children to care for and was also heavily pregnant, so she took the princesses and claimed sanctuary at Westminster Abbey. While there she gave birth to a son, whom she named Edward. This was joyous news for the Yorkist cause, as now Edward IV had a son and heir, and his dynasty appeared to have been blessed by God. In March 1471 Edward returned to England, landing at Hull, and led a campaign against the Lancastrian forces, which saw him defeat them first at the Battle of Barnet and then at the Battle of Tewkesbury.

Life in sanctuary was hard for the family, and while Elizabeth was only 5 years old at the time, it would have made a lasting impression on her. The abbey had grand living quarters and a manor house, called Cheyneygates, attached to it, so conditions were far from squalid, but the family would have been living in close quarters, and would not have been able to contact the outside world easily, or come by their usual foods, clothing or the other commodities they had become accustomed to as royals. They also would have been painfully aware that they were isolated and vulnerable, as the family of an ousted monarch, surrounded on all sides by those who denounced their legitimacy, marriage or even very existence.

By May 1471 though, Henry VI was dead, and Edward IV was restored to the throne. Elizabeth Woodville and her young family were reunited with their husband and father, and after months in sanctuary, they could return to their palaces and royal luxuries. Their reunion is remembered in a sweet poem written to commemorate the occasion:

The King comforted the Queen and other ladies eke,
His sweet babes full tenderly he did kiss;
The young Prince he beheld, and in his arms did bear;
Thus his bale turned him to bliss.
After sorrow, joy, the course of the world is.
The sight of his babes released part of his woe;
Thus the will of God in everything is do.[12]

The family quickly returned to normality as it had been before the brief hiatus in sanctuary. Elizabeth and her sisters welcomed more new siblings to the nursery, four sisters named Margaret, Anne, Catherine and Bridget, and two brothers, Richard and George.

Edward, as heir to the throne, was housed separately to his brothers and sisters, and instead of being sent to the nursery palaces alongside them, was set up with his own household as Prince of Wales. In 1473, at the age of just 2½, he was sent to Ludlow Castle in the Welsh Marches, and there he received training to prepare him for his future role as king. He was there to take up control of the Council of the Marches, which oversaw all the lands held in Wales. However, as the boy was merely an infant, the main purpose of this time was for him to receive training in all aspects of kingship, including a fully rounded education of the highest calibre.[13]

Although Edward's experience of childhood would have been very different to that of Elizabeth and her siblings, in others it was not so very dissimilar. The same aspirations were had of Elizabeth and her other brothers and sisters. As the highest-ranking noble family, they were expected to be well educated and prepared for their future roles in the nobility in England, and the girls particularly would have received tuition in court etiquette, foreign languages and other skills that would prepare them as future wives and ladies in foreign royal and noble houses. In 1474 a treaty was signed with Scotland to arrange the marriage of Princess Cecily, then only 5 years old, to Prince James of Scotland, the future James IV. He was only an infant at the time, so a proxy ceremony took place in Edinburgh to formalise the union.[14]

A year later in 1475, King Edward of England and Louis XI of France met at Picquigny to discuss peace between the two nations. As a part of this it was agreed that the Princess Elizabeth would be betrothed to the dauphin, Louis's eldest son, Charles.[15] Elizabeth was 9 years old when the treaty was signed and it was expected that she would go to France when she reached 'marriageable age', around 12. King Edward was particularly keen for the arrangements to be formalised as this was a major accomplishment for him as monarch. It was the first time that an English princess had married a French monarch, future or otherwise, and this deal brought with it status and respect in foreign diplomacy as well as a future strengthened alliance with one of the most powerful countries in Europe. However, when the time came that Elizabeth was considered old enough, King Louis of France stalled proceedings, claiming that his son, at 8 years old, was still too young to be wed; this led to the whole alliance being cast to the wind, and Elizabeth's marriage arrangements being cancelled.

Her younger siblings continued to make alliances; negotiations began for the marriage Edward, Prince of Wales with the Infanta Isabella of Spain, the eldest daughter of Ferdinand and Isabella, and Richard, Duke of York was married to Anne Mowbray, the heiress to the Duke of Norfolk. Her sisters made equally good matches into English noble houses, the Yorkist royal family were carving out alliances that would make them a powerhouse in European politics, but Elizabeth's future remained uncertain.

Elizabeth's future was unsettled because of her status as eldest daughter. Such was her connection to the throne that a marriage to her was considered a prize – both by her own family, and others who wanted influence over England. This point was seized upon by Henry when he announced his intention to marry her to unite the two houses, but it was also clear, following the disappearance of the Princes in the Tower, and his claiming of the throne of England away from Richard III, that Elizabeth would be the highest ranking, and therefore the most likely Yorkist claimant and heir to the throne. Had things gone differently, she could well have claimed the throne for herself – and she would have been Queen Elizabeth I instead of her granddaughter.

Elizabeth may not have wanted this, having witnessed the difficulties faced by her parents, particularly her mother. Having been banished into sanctuary during the time that Edward IV was in exile, and dealing with constant criticism about her lack of legitimacy as queen, Elizabeth Woodville also had the added pressures of producing heirs to the throne at a time when pregnancy, childbirth and infancy were incredibly dangerous undertakings. She did successfully give birth to ten children by the king and had already had two sons by her first marriage to Sir John Grey. This fecundity could be attributed to the fact that she came from a large family herself. Her mother, Jacquetta Woodville, had fourteen children, thirteen of whom survived childhood, so perhaps Elizabeth Woodville was not as scared of childbirth as some early-modern women would have been, but this did not mean there weren't losses or tragedies. Infant mortality rates were high in this period, and this did not change even for noble and royal families; childhood diseases, plagues and sicknesses were all prevalent and there was a certain degree of expectation that children might not survive infancy.

The first tragedy struck in 1472 when Elizabeth's sister – the family's youngest daughter – Margaret, died at just 8 months old. Elizabeth was just 6 at the time, but would have been keenly aware of the death of her little sister. A little over six years later, Prince George died at the age of 2, likely from plague, which was sweeping through the country at the time. The death of another child, and this time a son, would have hit the family hard, but especially the 13-year-old Elizabeth, who was of an age when she would be expected to marry and start a family of her own imminently. She would also have been the main support for her mother and may have been expected to shoulder more of the burden when dealing with grief than her sisters. Finally, in 1482, Elizabeth's closest sister, Mary, passed away after an illness. She had been Elizabeth's companion throughout her childhood, and her death, aged 14, must have been hard for them all to bear, but particularly for Elizabeth.

The sudden death of the king, Elizabeth's father, in 1483, followed by the disappearance of her two young brothers, alongside the family having to return to sanctuary once again, set them, the royal family and England into turmoil. Elizabeth found herself, for the second time in her short life, completely unsure about what her own future would hold, and with everything she had known up until this point in complete disarray. The only thing she and her family could do was to keep out of the way of the unfolding dramas and watch hopefully for a return to peace.

While Elizabeth and Henry, outwardly at least, appear to have had very different experiences of childhood and their younger years, they both knew from bitter experience about loss, heartbreak, disloyalty and threats to their safety. They had both grown up in the shadow of civil war and saw first-hand how life at court was simultaneously dangerous, disparate and dynamic.

Their similarities were as great as their differences though, as, as the daughter of privilege and having spent most of her life in a court setting, Elizabeth undoubtedly would have had higher expectations of what her life should be like, and a firmer grasp of the etiquette, rules and regulations that made up the life of royalty in a medieval royal palace. Henry, having been away from court, and from England, for almost his entire life, would not have had this knowledge, instead seeing threats and the moves and countermoves of the political situation more clearly than Elizabeth. Henry had been used to considerably more freedom, maybe not of movement per se, but of action. Life outside of court was altogether less driven by rules and traditions, and his life on the Continent may well have seemed more appealing than what was on offer in dreary, dilapidated England.

When Henry returned to England, he brought with him a great deal of experiences and a taste for finer things that England perhaps had not seen in many years of civil war. He had learned about art, drama, literature and other continental fashions while in exile, and these influences are evident in his actions, and the opportunities and experiences that he brings to his family and the wider court throughout his reign.

But both Henry and Elizabeth were bound by one thing: duty. Both had grown up knowing that their home, their family and their country all demanded respect and loyalty to the utmost of their being, and both would give their all in order to carry out their own personal duties, whatever those might be. They both took decisive action to ensure that whatever they did, their eventual aim was peace in England, and the joining of the warring factions that had brought so much instability to their lives.

The pair's concern for the future of the country is epitomised by the arrival of their first-born child, Prince Arthur, not quite nine months on from their wedding. To the two newlyweds this must have been joyous news – they had successfully done their duty and presented a child, an heir to the throne, as well as proven their compatibility with one another. To the outside world, it appeared that the marriage was a blessed one and that Henry's victory at Bosworth had been as God had intended.

Chapter 2

Prince Arthur

Following the wedding ceremony in January 1486, the royal couple remained in London and held court over celebrations in their honour, with spectacular banquets and dances. The celebrations were held all over London and further afield. As Bernard André describes:

> the most wished day of marriage was celebrated by them with all religious and glorious magnificence at court, and by their people, to show their gladness with bonfires, dancing, songs and banquets throughout all London, both men and women, rich and poor, beseeching God to bless the King and Queen and grant them a numerous progeny.[1]

This outpouring of support for the marriage of the king and queen was welcomed by all, especially by Henry and Elizabeth themselves, who knew just how important it was that their union, and rule, be accepted. It became apparent that their marriage represented the potential for peace in the form of an heir who would have their claims combined within him. Hall's Chronicle shows what was expected.

> By reason of whiche manage peace was thought to discende out of heaue into England, consideryng that the lynes of Lancastre & Yorke, being both noble families equiualet in ryches, fame and honour, were now brought into one knot and connexed together, of whose two bodyes one heyre might succede, which after their lyme should peaceably rule and enioye the whole monarchyand realme of England.[2]

Confident in their position early on, the king and queen worked to secure the future that so many hoped for and very soon after their wedding took place it was announced that the queen was with child. Whether that be out of duty, mutual respect, or genuine affection and love between them, the conception of a child was joyous news for all involved. Calculating from the date of their wedding, and Arthur's birth, it is reasonable to assume that they conceived quickly, if not on their wedding night itself. When Henry departed for a progress around Yorkshire and Lincolnshire in the early spring of 1486, he did not take Elizabeth with him, most likely because she was suffering from morning sickness, or other symptoms associated with the early stages of pregnancy. As a first-time mother, it would have been new to Elizabeth, but luckily, she had her experienced mother and mother-in-law both around to support her. While Henry was travelling, he sent regular letters to his new wife, and would send gifts to her while she stayed at the Palace of Placentia.

Elizabeth would have been familiar with the palace, having spent a lot of time there as a young girl. It would become one of the most favoured for the king and queen and would be renamed by Henry as Greenwich Palace. Both names emphasise how the palace was surrounded by green parks and fields, isolated from the hustle and bustle and potential diseases of London itself.

As soon as it could be confirmed that Elizabeth was with child, the wheels began turning to arrange yet more elaborate ceremony, intended to cement Elizabeth as queen, the Tudor dynasty as the ruling family, and rightfully on the throne. This started with Elizabeth's care while pregnant.

While it was not common for pregnant women to receive medical or ante-natal care in this period, Elizabeth's health would have been monitored and her diet checked, and healthy habits encouraged by her ladies and physicians. Pregnant women were discouraged from heavy activities or stressful situations, and sometimes forbidden to eat certain foods; for example, if a woman complained of morning sickness, she may be told to limit her intake of fish or milk, both of which modern doctors would recommend she eat.[3] Pregnancy was dangerous, as was childbirth, for both the mother and the child, so royal women were given the best possible conditions in which to give birth, according to the science of the time.

As a woman's due date got closer, she would be expected to enter confinement. This was a time where the pregnant woman and her household would isolate themselves in the woman's bedroom. Windows would be barred and draped, and air flow would be completely stifled as it was believed that illnesses were carried on the air. For a queen, preparations for confinement would be made by the king according to traditions laid out during the reign of Edward IV, Elizabeth's father. She would have been very familiar with the work that needed to be done, and the fact that the arrangements would be made for her by her husband.[4]

Henry took his role in arranging Elizabeth's confinement very seriously indeed. He purchased clothes and bedding for the chambers, all made of furs and velvet, and the most luxurious cotton sheets. He arranged for new furniture for her rooms and cushions stuffed with feathers, and even, bewilderingly, two velvet-covered saddles.[5]

However, by far the most important decision that Henry made regarding his wife's confinement and birth experience was to choose the location, and for Henry there was only one place that it could happen and that was the city of Winchester.

Winchester was important as it was believed to be the original city of Camelot, the place from which King Arthur and the knights of the round table ruled in the myths and legends that were so popular with people all over Europe, particularly with King Henry VII. In 1485, the printer William Caxton produced a first copy of Sir Thomas Mallory's *Le Morte D'Arthur*, a collection of all of the previous French and Middle English tales of King Arthur which had been popularised during the Middle Ages and early modern period. In *Le Morte D'Arthur* it is stated that the work was completed in 'the sixth year of King Edward IV', showing that the work had taken a long time, was readily available and well known enough to justify the mass printing of a collection of this type.[6]

Winchester had for a long time been identified as the potential site of Camelot and was the home of an artefact which was thought to be King Arthur's legendary round table. The table is still found in Winchester, mounted on the wall of the great hall of the castle, and now bears a painted surface showing a bright green and white patterning, and a central Tudor Rose.[7,8] This artwork, although added to by Henry VIII later in the century, was probably first applied by Henry VII to celebrate the arrival of their child, a son, whom they named Arthur.

The idea to have a prince born in Winchester and named Arthur was a well-planned and decisive statement about the status of the Tudor family on the throne. The Arthurian legends were well known, especially among the nobles upon which Henry relied on for support. The Arthurian legend includes a prophecy that King Arthur himself would return from Avalon to once again lead England. It was a powerful image for Henry to bestow onto his newborn son, that he was the returning King Arthur, the rightful leader and wearer of the English crown. It has even been speculated by historians that if Arthur had come to the throne he would have ruled as Arthur II, showing that he was truly the heir to Arthurian legacy.[9]

Henry didn't just project these identities onto his son however; he had also used Arthurian legend, and other prophecies linked with the king, to evidence and even exaggerate his own claim to the throne of England.

The Tudor family claimed to have links to several historical myths and legends, particularly within Welsh history. Their family lineage included Llywelyn the Great, the Prince of

Gwynedd, who had married King John's daughter, Joan, and taken over control of Wales as an independent principality. There were battles between Llywelyn and the lords who ruled over the Marches, and constant antagonism between Llywelyn in Wales and the kings of England. To the Tudors, Llywelyn proved their Welsh royal lineage and proved their rank in Welsh nobility.[10]

Going further back, they claimed to trace a line all the way to Cadwallader, the original Prince of Wales. He was king of Gwynedd in the seventh century and ruled over most of the area that is now North Wales. However, while we have little in the way of records about his life and rule, he is better known as a legendary character in history and mythology. In medieval literature mythology and history often intermingled, and this is the case when it comes to Cadwallader. For example, the Red Dragon of Wales, so well known for its prominence on the modern-day Welsh flag, is said to have been the symbol used by Cadwallader on his battle dress and banners; it was his heraldic symbol. This was adopted by Henry Tudor to use on his own heraldic banners on his journey to Bosworth, and then was integrated into the Royal Standard for the whole of the Tudor dynasty. However, there is no real evidence that Cadwallader used the dragon as his symbol, or that he was contemporarily known as 'the Red Dragon' by those who knew or fought him. This did not stop people writing about him in the centuries after from stating it as fact, and this is how and why it became such a powerful symbol for Henry Tudor and his progeny.[11]

One of the most well-known sources of this myth of the red dragon and for the significance of Cadwallader and

Llewellyn, was *The History of the Kings of Britain* by Geoffrey of Monmouth. His work tells the story of Britain's reigning kings from the inception of Britain by the soldier Brutus of Troy, all the way up to the time of his writing in the death of Cadwallader. According to Geoffrey, Brutus was given a prophetic vision by the goddess Diana, who told him:

> Brutus, beyond the setting of the sun, past the realms of Gaul, there lies an Island in the sea, once occupied by giants. Now it is empty and ready for your folk. Down the years this will prove an abode suited to you and to your people; and for you descendants it will be a second Troy. A race of Kings will be born there from your stock and the round circle of the whole earth will be subject to them.[12]

Brutus made the journey described in the vision, fighting seemingly everyone he met along the way, before he landed with his small group of followers on the shores of Britain, according to Geoffrey, at Totnes.[13] It is from Brutus that the island gained its name: 'Brutus then call the island Britain from his own name, and his companions the Britons … A little later the language of the people, which had up to that point been known as Trojan or Crooked Greek, was called British for the same reason.'[14]

In fact, other things have, legend has it, retained their links to Brutus and his original band of settlers. Geoffrey adds that his sons Kambrai and Albanactus lent their names to Wales and Scotland respectively, which is where the modern-day equivalents, Cymru and Alba, came from, and his follower Corineus gave his name to the Cornish and Cornwall.[15]

The line of descent goes, through the centuries, from Brutus and his descendants, to Uther Pendragon, father of King Arthur, who incidentally also came ashore at Totnes.[16] We are introduced to Merlin in the story and his prophecies relate to the Red Dragon, which represented the true British people:

> Alas for the Red Dragon, for its end is near. Its Cavernous dens shall be occupied by the White Dragon, which stands for the Saxons whom you have invited over. The Red Dragon represents the people of Britain, who will be overrun by the White One: for Britain's mountains and valleys shall be levelled, and the streams in its valleys shall run with blood.[17]

The Red Dragon was therefore an important symbol in British history, and with symbolism such as that described by Geoffrey, it is understandable that Henry Tudor would want to adopt a heraldic dragon – particularly a red one – which was linked to the people of Britain who were occupied and 'overrun' by a white force.

The Arthurian legend detailed by Geoffrey and other writers in the eleventh, twelfth and thirteenth centuries, however, was of probably the greatest importance to Henry. This was due in part to the Galfridian prophecy, which states that Arthur was not in fact killed, and would rise again to rule over his lands.

This idea had appeared in earlier writings, such as those by William of Malmesbury around the year 1125, who wrote: 'But Arthur's grave is nowhere seen, whence antiquity of fables still claims that he will return.'[18]

Geoffrey of Monmouth continued in this vein. In his version of Arthur's story, he writes: 'Arthur himself, our renowned king, was mortally wounded and was carried off to the Isle of Avalon, so that his wounds might be attended to.'[19] Arthur's fate is not clear here, and the myth that Arthur would return continues. There is even reference within the writings about Arthur that he was 'the fruit of the union of a red king and a white queen', which played into Henry's propaganda campaign almost too perfectly.[20]

Because of the popularity and common knowledge of both of these prophecies, it was in Henry Tudor's interest to use them to his advantage. Geoffrey's writings were commonly known, and the publication of *Le Morte D'Arthur* is evidence that the story was still very popular in fifteenth-century England, hundreds of years after Geoffrey and his contemporaries were writing about it. The work of Geoffrey of Monmouth was not without its critics however.

In around 1190, William of Newburgh wrote: 'it is quite clear that everything this man wrote about Arthur and his successors, or indeed about his predecessors from Vortigern onwards, was made up, partly by himself and partly by others'.[21] However, these voices were few and far between, and the legendary story of Arthur chimed with the popularity of history and romance that was so popular throughout Europe and across the whole of the medieval period.

There was also the interwoven prophecy that one day a Welshman would rise up to take the throne of England. This had been prevalent since Cadwallader's rule, and continued through Llywelyn's rule, and then was used again by Owain Glyn Dŵr during his revolt in 1414.[22] Glyn Dŵr had claimed the position of Prince of Wales and challenged the king for the right to rule over Welsh lands. Glyn Dŵr's revolution had not been so very long ago, so the prophecy of a Welshman taking the throne of England was still very much at the front of people's minds, especially in Wales.

Although there were other family members who already had the name Arthur (Arthur Plantagenet, Lord Lisle, was Elizabeth's half-brother and son of Edward IV, but no claim was made for him in the same way in regards to his name), to name the first-born son of a king Arthur was unusual. So, it is reasonable to assume that Henry had planned to name his first-born Arthur because it would link him irrevocably with the legend, would join England and Wales together under a 'Welsh' king, and solidify his claims to the throne through this heraldic symbolism.

And so, as soon as it was clear that Elizabeth was pregnant, plans were made for the birth. Once she was close enough to delivery to enter her confinement, the whole court would embark on a journey to Winchester, where they would stay until Arthur was born. His birth, in the city that was thought to have been the site of Camelot, was yet another carefully planned and highly symbolic act designed to reinforce the claim of Henry, and his son, to the throne.

Arthur was born on 20 September, most likely a little bit earlier than expected. His birth was eight months on from his parent's marriage, and it is unlikely that any form of consummation had happened prior to their wedding night. There is also evidence that his arrival was not expected at that point as the officials appointed as godparents were nowhere near Winchester at the time of his birth and had to hurry across the country in order to attend the ceremony of his baptism at Winchester Cathedral. The Earl of Oxford was at his home in Suffolk, entirely the other side of the country.

The ceremony took place four days after his birth. It was customary for the baptism to happen quickly, to welcome the child into the church, but in Prince Arthur's case it was even more important to introduce him to the country.

The baptism itself was a grand, highly choreographed affair and followed celebrations that had occurred in Winchester itself, where, after the announcement of Arthur's birth, the people of the city had lit fires and held celebrations involving food and copious amounts of drink. The birth of a son to the king and queen was a serious matter and so the ceremonials in the cathedral took on a formal and symbolic nature that aimed, once more, to cement the Tudor claim and make sure all those present knew that Arthur was the one true heir.

Nobles from all sides were involved in the ceremony, but high honours went to Sir Richard Woodville and Thomas

Brandon, from the king's household. Queen Elizabeth Woodville and a number of the queen's sisters were involved in the procession bringing the infant to the church. Arthur himself was held by his aunt, Princess Cecily, and Anne of York helped her with his clothing and robes during the ceremony.[23] The feasting after the ceremony took place in the great hall, and this is probably where the round table was used for its purpose of once again reiterating the Arthurian links to the Tudor dynasty. Throughout the ceremonies and celebrations, poetry and artworks were presented to the king which spoke about the foundations of the dynasty and drew on both the Arthurian legends and other medieval romances and classical myths. Musicians played and minstrels sang songs, all specially commissioned for the occasion.

Joyed may we be
Our Prince to see
And roses three.[24]

Prince Arthur's usefulness as a symbol of the future of Henry VII's reign did not end after his birth. He continued to be celebrated and admired, compared with classical characters, as the bringer of a Virgillian golden age, and quickly it was made clear that his parents, particularly his father, had high hopes for what was expected of him. His birth was also a physical manifestation of God's blessings, be it of Henry's ascension to the throne, the marriage of Henry and Elizabeth, or of a forthcoming Tudor dynasty. He was effectively a human version of the Tudor rose symbol and as such all of the hopes of his parents, and of the nation, rested in him.

Henry raised Arthur up from birth, bestowing the title of Duke of Cornwall as soon as he was born. Incidentally, this was also the title that was given by Henry VIII to his son, Henry. Unfortunately, the young Prince Henry lived for only six weeks, and the title was then passed on to others, but the title seems to have been something that would traditionally be passed on at this stage.

His nursery was initially set up alongside the queen's household, which remained in Winchester before the court returned to London in the Autumn of 1486. After this, a nursery was set up for him, separate from the royal households, and he had his own staff of servants, run by a chief nurse. Arthur's nurse for his first few years of his life was Lady Elizabeth Darcy, who had also served in the royal nursery under Edward IV and so would have been a familiar figure to the queen. She would have been able to trust the woman who had spent time with her and her siblings in their early years to give the very best to such an important infant. While it is likely he would have spent time at some of the main royal residences, Prince Arthur's household would have lived separately from his parent's households. His first formal home was at Farnham Castle in Surrey, which is little more than a day's ride from the city, but would have been in a safe, rural location for the prince to grow and learn.[25]

It wasn't long before Arthur's position as the heir to the throne became useful to the king once more. At the tender age of 18 months, negotiations began between Henry's envoys and those of Ferdinand and Isabella of Spain. It was intended that Arthur would have a Spanish bride, the 'infanta' Catherine of Aragon, youngest daughter of the Spanish monarchs. Negotiations went well and in 1489 the two countries signed the Treaty of Medina del Campo, bringing England and Spain into an alliance that would have far reaching consequences.[26] The alliance was of great importance to Henry. This was the first time that a major international power had made an alliance with England since he had taken the throne. Their signatures on the treaty meant that, at least in some way, he was recognised as king on an international stage. Alliances with major powers were, just as they are now, mutually beneficial economically and militarily and, despite Henry's changes to the taxation system, he was still enduring issues with lack of funds, and was fighting off pretenders and challengers to his throne. With the backing of Spain it was perhaps felt that his position would become – at least a little bit – less precarious.

Around this same time as negotiations were concluding with Spain, Queen Elizabeth fell pregnant again and it seems that the king felt it was a good time for Arthur to take a step up from his nursery and start his preparations for his future role as king. On 29 November 1489, the day after his baby sister was born, Arthur was made Earl of Chester and Prince of Wales and granted his estates on the Marches of Wales.[27] It was planned that he would take control of the Council of the Marches, but Arthur was only 3 years old at this point so the council was handed over to his uncle, Jasper Tudor, until Arthur was old enough to be given authority. He was to take up residence in the

Marches and to learn from his tutors there, while overseeing and learning about the management of this often-fractious area of the British Isles.

Arthur spent time at Tickenhill, near Bewdley in Shropshire, and at Ludlow Castle. Ludlow was the main meeting place for the council and the official residence of the Prince of Wales, and had been where Edward IV had sent his son Edward while he was Prince of Wales also. In the same way that Prince Edward had lived in Ludlow with a household of tutors and responsible adults, so Prince Arthur had the same given to him. It could be that Elizabeth was influential in this decision, having witnessed her brother's experience as Prince of Wales, and perhaps advising Henry as to what was expected or what could be done differently.

There were certainly similarities between Arthur's experience and that of his uncle Edward. He was given tutors and had people around him who valued academic excellence as well as more traditional kingly or knightly skills. Edward had had the queen's brother, Anthony Woodville, who had been a well-known scholar and had a reputation as a sophisticate. Arthur had a number of tutors, mostly humanist in their outlook, including Bernard André and Master John Rede, who taught him languages, classics and scripture. Arthur seems to have been a capable pupil and according to André's lists of the books used in his tuition, he would have been familiar with philosophers and historians such as Ovid and Tacitus, and also had a reputation for his sporting, hunting and archery skills.[28]

This type of education was following the new humanist style of learning, and by employing tutors such as André, who followed these ideas, Arthur was being prepared to enter a modern European political sphere.

As well as tutors and guardians, there were also boys his own age to keep him company. Arthur's household included sons of noblemen who joined him in his studies and served him in his chambers. Some were from English families who were proven loyal to Henry and his reign, and others had Welsh connections such as Gruffydd ap Rhys ap Thomas, the son of a Welsh ally of Henry's, who would go on to be Arthur's friend until his death. This connection to Wales could well have been Henry's will in action, imitating his own experience of growing up in the Marches, encouraging knowledge of their Welsh heritage, and bringing Arthur closer to the Welsh nobles he would one day have to rule over.

All these experiences were intended to prepare Arthur to one day inherit the throne from his father. By giving Arthur a modern, European-influenced education and experience of dealing with a difficult political landscape, Henry probably hoped that his son would be able to take up the reins with no problems, and certainly be better prepared than he was when he landed his ships in Pembrokeshire.

Attendance at court also helped prepare Arthur for rule, though this did not happen often in his early years. King and queen did not want to expose their infant son to disease and other dangers present in London and at court, and this meant his visits were infrequent. However, there were times that the royal households merged and came together, and these times normally involved celebrations. Christmas and New Year, Easter, religious festivals, marriages, official visits, and probably most significantly for Arthur and his family, the births of more royal children.

Chapter 3

Margaret, Henry, and Elizabeth

The birth of a baby girl on 28 November 1489 was once again a joyous occasion at the court. Her pregnancy was confirmed in the summer of 1489, but this time Elizabeth stayed in London for her confinement and gave birth at the Palace of Westminster. Even though Margaret's gender may well have been a slight disappointment to those who sought a second prince to bolster the family lines, Margaret was given all the pomp and ceremony befitting a princess for the baptism which took place on 30 November, in St Stephen's Chapel of the palace. Just like Arthur's before, the whole court was present, and her Woodville relatives took centre stage leading the procession which made its way through Westminster Hall in full view of the court.[1]

She was named Margaret, most logically after her paternal grandmother, Margaret Beaufort, who also stood as her godparent at the ceremony. The name Margaret had been long used by royal and noble families and so it would have been deemed very suitable. Her grandmother also took on most of the responsibility for the preparations for the christening, arranging the robes and furs for the new princess to wear, and organising the officials in attendance. She even made arrangements for the font from Canterbury Cathedral to be transported up ready to be used in the ceremony. This font had been used for the baptisms of royal children 'for as long as anyone could remember', as historian Maria Perry describes it, and so this was an important symbol of Princess Margaret's status as the eldest daughter of the king.[2]

Perhaps as well as Margaret Beaufort's hand at work, we can also see Queen Elizabeth's influence. She would be familiar with the traditions associated with royal children and would have seen her siblings being christened and welcomed into the royal household. While she would have been unable to attend the ceremony itself, that does not mean that she did not help to plan, make arrangements, and make requests for certain aspects to be implemented.

All of the ceremony and celebration of that November, the arrival of the princess and the investiture of Arthur as Prince of Wales, gives an impression of normality and calm in England in 1489. The family was growing, celebrating the milestones of married life and of rule, but the country was far from peaceful. The royal family were under pressure from threats, both domestic and further afield. The pretender Lambert Simnel and the associated rebellion had only been stopped in 1487 by Henry's victory at the Battle of Stoke, but some of those who had supported Simnel were still at large, both at court and on the Continent. Margaret of York was still a presence in Burgundy, and she would consistently back opponents of Henry in attempts to further the Yorkist cause. Other claimants still existed within the noble families in England and, despite being mostly supported by the court, there was always a risk that they would decide to oppose him, and this meant that Henry forever had to be watchful and suspicious.

For all of these reasons it was imperative that Henry and Elizabeth secure their throne further. The political alliance with Spain had helped steady the ship in some ways, but what was really needed was another male heir, who would secure the line of succession and cast doubt about the certainty of the Tudor claim to the English throne into the shadows.

In the spring of 1491, a little over a year after Margaret's birth, Elizabeth entered confinement once more. This time, to the joy of all involved, it was a boy. He was born on 28 June 1491, and was named Henry, after his father. This time Elizabeth chose to give birth at the Palace of Placentia, and perhaps this was to avoid all of the clamour that was associated with the palaces in the centre of the city. In the middle of summer there could have been plague or sweating sickness that could have threatened the newborn baby. As we have already discussed though, Placentia was one of the Elizabeth's old nursery palaces from when she was a child, and perhaps this meant that she felt safe and secure in familiar surroundings for her third birth experience.

Prince Henry was presented to the court at his baptism, just days after his birth, just as his siblings had been before him. He was taken to the nearby church, which was the home to the Observant Franciscans, and was baptised by the Bishop of Exeter, Richard Fox.[3] The whole court would have been called to attend, but the church was not a particularly large one, so the guest list was probably not as long as it had been for the baptisms of Arthur or Margaret. A second son would have been greeted with great joy though, so it is easy to imagine that there were grand feasts in the palace to welcome the new prince.

A little more than a year later and there was more cause for celebration. Another princess, this time named Elizabeth, for her mother and grandmother, joined the family. She was born at Sheen Palace, on 2 July 1492, and while we have very little in the way of records about her early days, she would have been welcomed in a similar fashion to her brothers and sister. As a fourth child, and a daughter at that, the celebrations may have been more muted or less extravagant, but her birth would still have been a very welcome addition to the Tudor family.

Elizabeth had given birth to four children in four different places, all within six years. She had produced two sons and heirs for Henry to continue the Tudor dynasty, and two daughters whose marriages could be used to further England on the international stage through marriage treaties. For Elizabeth and for Henry, the children represented the completion of the formation of a new royal family, and to bring peace to the country through the knowledge that these children were true heirs to the throne, and could not be challenged.

All of the children, not just Prince Arthur, were seen as an embodiment of the joining of the warring factions, the houses of Lancaster and York, the red and white roses. This imagery was used throughout their lives, in poetry and in artworks that were associated with them. When Margaret was married to James IV of Scotland, poems were commissioned that presented her as a rose 'of colour red and white' and the poem continues:

…Hail, be thou, richest Rose!
Hail, herbs' Empress! Hail, freshest Queen of Flowers![4]

The reference to Prince Henry being this joining of the roses became even more common after the death of his brother, Prince Arthur. John Skelton's poetry includes lines that are explicit in their images.

O, noble Prince Henry! Our second treasure,
Surmounting in virtue and mirror of beauty!
O, gem of gentleness and lantern of pleasure!
O, rubicund blossom and star of humility!
O, famous bud, full of benignity![5]

When Henry inherited the throne from his father, Skelton's poetry stepped up the imagery further. The opening of his poem *A lawde and prayse made for our sovereign lord the king* makes the reference to the Tudor rose very clear indeed:

The rose both white and Red
In one Rose nowe doth grow;
Thus thorow every stede
There of the same dothe blow:
Grace and sede did sow.[6]

There is another example from 1511, when his son, Henry, was born. A poem was written to be included in the records known as *The Great Tournament Rose of Westminster*, showing the same sort of image to underpin his claim and legitimacy:

> Oure ryall Rose now Reignyng rede and Whyte
> Sure graftyd is on grounde of nobylnes
> In harry the VIII our ioye and our delyte
> Subdewer of wronge mayntenar or rightwysnes.[7]

The giving of titles and the performance of duties, particularly at special occasions, were also ways to give legitimacy and acknowledgement at court. Prince Henry, just as his older brother had done, received titles and was granted lands at an early age. At just under 2 years old he was made the Constable of Dover Castle, and then aged 3, Lieutenant of Ireland. On 30 October 1494, Prince Henry took part in a ceremony that made him a member of the Order of the Bath, an ancient order of knights, closest to the king. In the ceremony other nobles had to help the 3-year-old to fulfil certain parts of the ceremony, including the Earl of Shrewsbury, who had to carry the toddler, and the Duke of Buckingham, who placed a spur on Henry's right foot. The next day more ceremonies were held where King Henry, in front of all of the assembled nobles and in full royal regalia, officially proclaimed his son as Duke of York.[8] This meant that Prince Henry was considered a member of the ruling elite, even if it was only a title at such a young age, and this bolstered his position as a second prince, and an important member of the family.

While the girls didn't have any titles to their names directly, it was their destiny to marry according to the wishes of their father and so they were often included in ceremonies for special occasions, and would attend court for festivities so that they may be presented to ambassadors, potential suitors and generally shown off. While a son showed a strong throne and a good chance of domestic stability, daughters could represent huge strides in international diplomacy. Two boys and two girls gave the family security for the future, at a time when infant mortality was high and childbirth was risky, their survival was highly protected – and remarkable when viewed with the statistics.

The children themselves were an important symbol for Henry and Elizabeth too. Four children in six years was proof enough for some that the family was indeed blessed in God's eyes; that they were meant to be on the throne, and that their family was, according to God's plan, destined to rule. For this reason the king and queen were involved parents, and protected and provided for their children, investing time, money and resources in them. In accounts for Elizabeth's personal household expenses we can see regular payments for clothing and winter coats for the children, especially the girls, and to their nurses and other staff.

A later entry in the books speaks of: 'to the said Lady Bray for money by her given to a Scottish man scole-master to the prince at his departure.'[9] This insight shows that Elizabeth was taking a hands-on approach to her parenting responsibilities and was involved in ensuring that the royal nursery ran smoothly.

The three younger children, all born within a space of four years, formed the family nursery and appear to have shared a close bond. They spent most of their time together, in the care of their nurses and, later, their tutors. The royal nursery was not in one place but was a household unto itself which travelled with the court some of the time, or moved to be closer to the court for occasions or festivals such as Christmas and New Year celebrations. There are records showing that the royal children spent time at the palaces at Sheen, Greenwich (the new name for the Palace of Placentia) and Westminster, but a lot of the time they were housed in the royal palace at Eltham. These were the same houses and palaces that Elizabeth had grown up in and would have been familiar to her and her relatives; perhaps she was comforted to know that her children were in the places where she had spent her childhood. The palaces were close enough to London that Elizabeth and Henry would be able to visit, or request that the children be brought to them, without it being a long or dangerous journey.

As already discussed, Arthur's household was separate to the nursery of his siblings. He spent most of his time at places such as Farnham, and then further afield in the Midlands and Welsh borders. Arthur wasn't quite 6 years old when Elizabeth was born, so the nursery setup would though have been similar in both households, and perhaps Arthur would have joined his siblings when they all attended events at court, or just for family visits. There is nothing to suggest that they were kept apart for any other reason than Arthur's preparation for kingship, so it is conceivable that they would have crossed paths frequently for family events.

The four children seem to have been enough for Elizabeth and Henry. They were all being well taken care of, all healthy and happy, and appeared to bring the same joy to their parents as they did to the nation. The family of six made up the new house of Tudor, and the future seemed bright.

Chapter 4

The Royal Nursery

Children in the royal nursery were not treated particularly differently to any child from a noble or wealthy family, and this included a practice common among most women in these circumstances, the hiring of a wet nurse to feed their newborn infant, usually for the first year of their life.[1] Wet nurses were normally people who were familiar to the family, and who lived nearby. For a royal child, the wet nurse would have lived with the family, enabling them to attend to the baby in a nursery environment. However, it was not unusual for other families to send their baby to live with their nurse in their homes. This allowed the wet nurse to attend to the child while also running their own home. Some wet nurses were married and had children of their own, as was the case for Thomas More and his wife Joanna, who sent their daughter Margaret to live with her wet nurse, Mistress Giggs.[2]

We know that the royal nursery was staffed by women from noble families or by local gentlewomen, and staff would move from palace to palace, and from baby to baby as they were born, taking on their specific roles in caring for each child, for example Prince Arthur's carer, Alice Bywimble, moved over to care for Prince Henry around the time of his birth in June 1491.[3] Princess Margaret's rocker, Margaret Traughton, moved to care for the new-born Prince Henry, but Margaret's nurse, Alice Davy, stayed with her, as did her other nurses, Anne Mayland and Margaret Gower. Prince Henry's rockers would remain with him also and he even invited his wet nurse, Anne Oxenbridge, to attend his coronation as an adult. This kind of attachment was common, as a bond would be made between the child and the nurses, as well as a trusting relationship between the nurses and the parents. All of them would form a team in caring for these important children.[4]

However, having a wet nurse was contrary to the guidance that was given to mothers and, just as today, breast was considered best. In *The Byrth of Mankynd* by Richard Jonas, the most popular book on midwifery in the period, he says 'for because that in the mothers bellye it was wonte to the same and feede with it', meaning that the mother should provide what the baby was used to during the pregnancy, after the birth and continuing through infancy.[5]

The reason wet nurses were popular was that, for noble women, it was more important that they were able to keep their roles at court, to maintain their positions and help their husbands with their work, and to increase the possibility of another pregnancy quickly. If a mother continued to breastfeed, the likelihood of another pregnancy would decrease, and so it was considered par for the course that a royal mother would employ a wet nurse and other people to look after their children while they carried out their court, and familial, responsibilities.

Another big reason for this drive to have more babies was due to the high infant mortality rate. This was an ever-present danger to parents of young children and would have driven royal mothers to try to have more children, in order to protect their family line. For the period of 1500–1599, it is thought that the mortality rate was around 13 per cent of all children died before their first birthday, and then another 6 per cent for children under 4 years of age.[6] This also explains why the children were kept separate from the rest of the family, from the court, and also in rural environments which were believed to be healthier for them.

Prince Arthur was taken quickly away from his mother and the court and was set up in his nursery at Farnham Castle in Surrey. He was put under the care of nurses and governesses, some of whom were previously nurse to Elizabeth and her siblings when they were young. This is our first indication of Elizabeth's investment and interest in her children's upbringing. Henry, as we have seen previously, did not have a normal experience of childhood, particularly a royal childhood, whereas Elizabeth did. She had been brought up as a princess of England, and apart from the short spell she and her mother and siblings spent in sanctuary in Westminster in 1470–1471, she was well used to how a royal nursery should be run and what was expected of herself and Henry, the staff and also the children.

However, once Arthur was sent to the Welsh Marches, the arrangements for him completely changed compared with those for his siblings. Although they were set up in a similar nursery environment, unlike Arthur, who lived a comparatively solitary existence, the three siblings would spend a lot of time in one another's company. Their time was split between palaces, with Eltham being the main home, again probably because of its proximity to London, as well as possibly being seen as a sentimental or traditional place. The children were the responsibility of a staff of nurses and maids, all of whom would see to their every need.

In the children's early years this meant mainly dealing with their clothing and cleanliness, teaching them basic skills such as manners and etiquette, and learning through play – very similar to how young children would be brought up in any household.[7] Although writing a little later, around the year 1608, the author and paediatrician William Perkins said: 'the first instruction of children in learning and religion must be so ordered that they may take it with delight. For which purpose, they may be sometimes allowed in moderate manner to play and solace themselves in recreations fitting for their years.'[8] Perkins had translated his work from an earlier piece, originally written in French, and had been one of a number of guidance books intended to help families, especially those who were ambitious and wished for their families to rise through the ranks, raise their children. These guides included all sorts of advice, including how children should be educated, and were used by parents at all levels of society. Because of this, the importance of learning through play may well have been an attitude common in nurseries throughout England, including that of the royal family. Children would have been given opportunities to play and to learn from their mothers and from those who were responsible for their care, but their formal education would not begin until they were a little older, and capable of learning in a more academic way.

However, the royal children were expected to be present at formal occasions, even at quite a young age, and perhaps this led to their home environment being a little bit more formal and structured to foster those skills and reflect the life they were going to have as they got older. An example of this was when 3-year-old Prince Henry was invested as the Duke of York. The celebrations for this momentous occasion were immense and involved the whole court, including Prince Henry at the centre, and 5-year-old Princess Margaret, who stood at her mother's side and took a leading role in the ceremonies.

Before the ceremony, Prince Henry was led in a great procession and was received by statemen including the Mayor of London and his aldermen. Prince Henry was present at the feast that followed, not to eat but to hold the towel with which his father, the king, would wipe his hands while he ate. This was a huge honour in of itself, but for a 3-year-old child, it must have been a daunting and massive undertaking. Margaret was given the honour of awarding the prizes at the tournament that followed all the formal ceremonies, and the crowds were delighted to see her. Accounts of the day describes how they celebrated and shouted about 'the redoubted lady, the fairest young princess, the eldest daughter to our sovereign lord the King'.[9]

While the children were active in some parts of court life, they wouldn't have seen their parents every day, and they wouldn't have been physically close to their parents most of the time. Their mother and father would visit them often in the nursery, and the children would be expected to greet them as monarchs, not necessarily fondly as parents, but this does not mean that there was not affection or attention given by Henry and Elizabeth to their offspring.

Due to the distances that often separated them, both Henry and Elizabeth would send letters to their children, and to their nurses and carers, to keep abreast of what was going on in their children's lives. The children themselves would have been encouraged to write to their parents once they were old enough to read and write, and samples of their schoolwork would have been sent to show their progress, just as today's children bring home artwork and school reports.

Henry and Elizabeth were also generous with gifts, particularly of clothes. Elizabeth's records show that she would regularly send fabric to be made into clothes for the children, or items such as gloves, hose and other garments for the children.[10] As with most young children, their clothing and other necessities ultimately fell under the mother's responsibility, and Elizabeth was no different in this respect, but she and Henry would also pay for more frivolity and fun for the children. In Elizabeth's records we can see payments made for Easter gifts for the children and for clothes for the children of others, such as the those of Henry Courtenay.[11] We also see in records that Elizabeth paid for musicians, minstrels and other entertainment for her household. On 24 March 1502 she paid 3s and 4d 'to a mynstrell that played upon a droon before the Quene at Richemount in re-warde'.[12] It is likely that these types of entertainers would have been sent on to entertain the children or brought in to the household when the children were present, so that they could be shared between her and the rest of the family.

We have less evidence of Henry's involvement in the children's life. His record keeping was impeccable, but the expectation of the children's household being run as a separate entity meant that his fingerprint was not often on purchases or decisions. In some records of accounts listing expenses, payments are seen to be made to the household of 'our right dearly beloved well-beloved children the Lord Henry the Ladies Margaret and Elizabeth', payments included salaries for the staff and for the upkeep of the buildings themselves, but without much in the way of detail.[13]

However, later letters between himself and his children show a level of attachment to them, and other people who would become important to his family and their roles as royals. We have letters from Henry to Arthur, to Catherine of Aragon, to Princess Margaret, all of whom were living away from court for prolonged periods and were old enough to respond to him.[14] Henry may not have had much time to spend with his children, especially in the early years of his reign while he dealt with the responsibilities of being king, but his interest in them, their lives, and their futures is undeniable.

One way in which Henry may have had a greater level of influence, was in the children's religious education. For Henry, as for most people in this period, the Christian faith was central to everyday life. The calendar revolved around religious festivals and church ceremonies, and prayers dominated daily life and weekly routines. Henry, though, was particularly focused on piety in his life and gave generously to churches and to colleges for theological study. John Guy describes Henry as 'conventionally, even ostentatiously pious', which shows that perhaps, more than others, the king made a show of his faith. Guy speculates that perhaps this was more for show and that 'piety was a useful prop to his status'.[15] However, his mother Margaret Beaufort was extremely pious too; she was a great supporter of religious houses and institutions, and was highly influential in her son's religious life and decisions when he was king. Henry was dedicated to his faith, and even supported the followers of his predecessor, Henry VI, who was starting to be seen as a saint-like figure with miracles attributed to him and his tomb in Windsor. It was Henry Tudor who built a chapel at Westminster Abbey to house relics attributed to him.[16]

Religious education was the main thing that was taught to children prior to 'formal' education beginning. As well as teaching children about their faith, and how to behave in the many important ceremonies and celebrations that happened regularly, it was a conduit for all the skills they would need later for more academic learning and was also way to teach manners and morals from a young age.[17] While it was usually the mother who would instruct young children in their first lessons in religion, given Henry's own interest in religion and how important faith was to him, and to his mother, it is plausible that it was Henry, as well as Elizabeth and Margaret, who made sure that the children received the very best standard of religious education.

Up to the age of about 7, both boys and girls were treated similarly even in the more formal royal household. The children would have the same expectations for behaviour and would even be dressed in similar styles of clothing.[18] While Arthur's experiences were different due to his position as heir, his care and the things he was taught prior to his move to Ludlow would have been the same in most ways as that of his siblings.

Henry, in a similar way to Arthur, took on a role of leader, and the nursery is often referred to as the 'lord Prince's household', implying that Henry was perhaps considered the most important resident of the nursery.[19] However, the thing that made this little nursery special was the closeness of the children who lived there. Margaret, Henry and Elizabeth formed a little group, who would do more or less everything together. They grew close and loyal to one another, and Henry as the only boy took his role in the group as his sisters' protector very seriously indeed.

Chapter 5

Education and Preparation

When Arthur was sent to Ludlow he began, at the early age of 3, a more formal plan of learning. This was a little younger than would have been usual for children generally, but royal children would begin earlier and usually when they were deemed capable, rather than waiting for an arbitrary age or stage.[1] When Princess Margaret was born, Arthur's position changed almost immediately and so he was sent to begin his preparations for kingship, while his sister, and the other siblings that followed, would continue in the nursery setting. Margaret, and Henry who followed less than two years later, would have started their education anytime from around 4 because, just like their brother, their parents held high expectations for them to achieve great things.

Once their formal learning began, they would have spent their days having lessons with tutors, being taught all the skills and knowledge that was seen as necessary for young nobles and courtiers. This included subjects such as foreign languages including French and Latin, mathematics, some sciences such as astronomy, reading classical literature to learn history and political thinking, and learning scripture. They would also learn how to play musical instruments, dance, play sports, ride horses, and partake in skills such as archery, hawking and other aristocratic pastimes. Margaret had a reputation as a skilled hunter and archer, and on a hunting trip during her progress to Scotland, she impressed the assembled nobles when she shot what was described as 'a fine buck'.[2]

It was traditional that the boys would learn more of the physical or knightly skills, but up until later in their adolescence their physical education was mainly kept to a gentle pace. This was because it was believed that too much exertion would damage the growing body and stunt growth and development.[3] Training in knightly or military skills would not begin until at least 14, or some as late as 16, although these skills were first introduced in the nursery through toys and play, especially in boys of noble backgrounds for whom service in the military would be expected.

Physical activities were also encouraged for girls, again encouraging physical fitness without overexerting themselves and potentially damaging their bodies. For girls, though, the main emphasis was on gentility and courtly diplomacy. The same subjects, such as languages and scripture would serve a noblewoman well in making a good marriage or fulfilling a role at court as a lady-in-waiting for example. For Margaret, Elizabeth and, later on, Mary, and other princesses in this period, plans for their future would have begun at a very early age. Margaret would have known from around 3 years of age that there were plans for her to be married to the king of Scotland, and negotiations were underway for a marriage for Elizabeth when she was older.

It was these early negotiations and expectations that meant it was important they were prepared for any eventuality, and it was important that girls, as well as boys, were educated. However, it would have been a generalised preparation until plans were formalised and even then, girls were not expected to have as thorough or as in-depth an education as their male siblings and counterparts; gentility and femininity would have been more important than educational excellence.

However, influences from Europe and from newer renaissance fashions meant that a new style of education became popular, and from the middle of the fifteenth century both the boys and the girls were given the opportunity to cover skills and topics that ordinarily would not have been considered important. Just as we have discussed with Anthony Woodville's influence on the education of the young Edward V, there was also a humanist and renaissance influence on the education of Henry and Elizabeth's children. We can see this in the decisions they made and, particularly, in the tutors they chose to employ to educate their sons and daughters.

Elizabeth's uncle, Anthony Woodville, was able to influence the education of her younger brother and although she had no formal education herself, she would have benefited from being close to this while growing up. As a young woman, she in turn was able to influence decisions on the education of her own children, both sons and daughters, for their future roles in the family.

In a similar vein, Margaret Beaufort was herself well-educated, though not in a formal way, and perhaps spoke up for her grandchildren to receive the very best of educational provision available, in the same way that she may well have done for her son. Henry himself knew, from the experience of his own education and his time on the Continent before he became king, that modern educational practices could be beneficial to his own children. Particularly that of the most fashionable, and in some ways more controversial, humanist ways.

Humanism was a school or group of ideas which focused on education and learning as a way to be closer to God, and to be a better Christian. By looking at scholarship from classical literature and scripture, and learning language and writing skills, a person could have a deeper understanding of humanity and how best to serve God while they are on earth. The ideas began in continental Europe with theologians and philosophers such as Desiderius Erasmus, and their writings influenced others and inspired numerous scholars including Martin Luther, Sir Thomas More and others who were employed by the English king at court. A number were employed as tutors for Arthur and his siblings in their respective nurseries and this influenced the type of education they received, making it more modern and in greater depth, for both the boys and the girls, than previous generations of royal children.

As noted, one of Arthur's tutors was Bernard André, a humanist as well as a poet who was employed by King Henry to write poetry and record events occurring at the English court. He was brought to court when Henry became king and remained a loyal member of the king's retinue up until his death, receiving an annual pension in return for writing an official annual summary of events.[4] Arguably, however, André's most important and influential role was as Prince Arthur's tutor, where he was responsible for designing Arthur's curriculum and also ensuring he learned everything he needed as Henry's heir. André kept records of the curriculum he designed and lists of everything that Arthur learned from, read or was taught. On this list were classical scholars including Cicero, Homer, Ovid and Virgil, and according to André, Prince Arthur had 'either committed them partly to memory or, with his own hands and eyes, had read them often and considered them'.[5] All of André's writing on the subject means that we have a fairly good idea of the kinds of things that Arthur, and later Prince Henry, would have been expected to know.

Prince Henry's tutors also had a humanist and renaissance influence to their style. One of his tutors was John Skelton, another court poet and scholar who produced work for Henry VII throughout his reign. He was tutor to Prince Henry, but in all likelihood was tutor to Princess Margaret also, as well as Princess Mary later on.[6] He concentrated on classical scholarship also, and Prince Henry appears to have had a natural talent for Latin and other languages as well as theology and philosophy. Skelton notes that around the age of 16, Prince Henry was familiar with a large collection of Latin texts, but does not appear to have owned copies of English translations which would have been available to him in the royal libraries. These translations had been produced for Edward of Westminster, son of Henry VI but, impressively, Prince Henry did not need them in order to read or learn from the texts.[7]

Another influence on Prince Henry was Arthur Plantagenet. Arthur was the half-brother of Elizabeth of York, son of Edward IV and his mistress Elizabeth Wayte. While Arthur was not recognised as a part of the royal family, he was elevated to Lord Lisle by Henry VII; given responsibilities and lands, he would eventually be put in charge of the English port of Calais.[8] However, at the time when his half-sister was queen he was a member of her household and would have been a regular visitor to the royal nursery to see his nephews and nieces. While his educational background isn't well known, he was brought up around the court of his father and would have been a great source of information for the children in the nursery and may have helped, particularly Prince Henry, with knightly skills and masculine expectations, providing him with a male role model while in the more feminine surroundings of the nursery. He may also have helped with things like horse-riding and hunting skills, again things that Prince Henry and Princess Margaret would need to learn, but that members of their household may not have been well-placed to teach. However, there is evidence to suggest that Lord Lisle's interest in education did not just lie in practical skills and the more playful style of interactions. From his two marriages he had three daughters and stepchildren, all of whom he helped and encouraged in their own education, and his interactions with the royal nursery may have inspired this.

Another humanist who was linked to the royal court and to the education of the royal children was William Blount, Baron Mountjoy. He was a lawyer, trained at Lincoln's Inn in London where he gained connections to court and to his humanist circles.

Blount had also studied in Europe, had been heavily influenced by Italian and French scholarship, and counted Sir Thomas More among his acquaintances. This mutual interest led to Thomas and other young lawyers being invited to Eltham Palace to visit the nursery and meet the young Princess Margaret and Prince Henry, as well as the other royal children. Thomas brought with him another humanist acquaintance, and a man who would go on to shape the humanist world, Desiderius Erasmus.

The visit took place in 1499, and Erasmus was not expecting to meet with Blount, or indeed the royal children. He wrote about the meeting:

> I was staying at lord Mountjoy's country house when Thomas More came to see me, and took me out with him for a walk as far as the next village, where all the king's children except Prince Arthur … were being educated. When we came into the hall, the attendants not only of the palace but also of Mountjoy's household were all assembled. In the midst stood prince Henry, then nine years old, and having already something of royalty in his demeanour, in which there was a certain dignity combined with singular courtesy. More … presented [Henry] with some writing. For my part, not having expected anything of the sort, I had nothing to offer, but promised that on another occasion I would in some way declare my duty towards him. Meanwhile I was angry with More for not having warned me, especially as the boy sent me a little note, while we were

> at dinner, to challenge something from my pen. I went home, and in the Muses' spite, from whom I had been so long divorced, finished the poem within three days.[9]

Blount's influence on his students was therefore profound and offered a new way of thinking and learning, exposed the children to new ideas, as well as bringing in scholars to meet them directly, which was not something that, for example Prince Arthur, was able to experience while he was isolated in his household at Ludlow.

As well as adult visitors, the children had visitors and companions at the nursery, some of whom would stay for prolonged periods and become great friends for their whole lives. Just as Arthur had had the children of Welsh nobles come to live and study with him, the other children had companions in their studies, brought in from other noble families, either related to the king or the queen, or in need of the king and queen's support. Perhaps the most famous of these was Charles Brandon, who would later go on to be elevated to become the Duke of Suffolk and marry Princess Mary. Charles came to the royal household when he was placed as a ward of the king following his father's death at the Battle of Bosworth. Sir William Brandon was loyal to Henry Tudor, following him throughout his journey and carrying the standard onto the battlefield at Bosworth. In *The Ballad of Bosworth*, an anonymous poem telling the story of the battle, Sir William is mentioned by name:

among all other Knights, remember
which were hardy, & therto wight;
Sir William Brandon was one of those,
King Heneryes Standard he kept on height[10]

Following his father's death, Henry Tudor took Charles on in the household and gave him an education, feeding him and clothing him, raising him alongside the royal children. Charles was born c.1484, so he was a little older than Prince Henry and the rest of the children, but they appear to have gotten along extremely well. Later in life he is described as 'a person comely of stature, high of courage and conformity of disposition to King Henry VIII, with whom he became a great favourite'.[11]

Another name who is mentioned as being present in the nursery alongside the children is a girl who goes by the name of Jane Poppincourt. The girls most probably met when Mary spent time at Margaret Beaufort's household and Maria Perry says that Jane 'seems to have been one of Mary's companions from earliest childhood'.[12] Jane appears, in a similar way to Charles Brandon for Prince Henry, throughout Mary's life; when Mary left to go to France, Jane was one of the ladies who accompanied her, and later on Jane is mentioned by Mary when she is back in England. Jane may well have kept Mary company while her older siblings were away from the nursery or fulfilling their obligations at court.

As the children got older, there were more and more expectations of them. Mary was younger, and therefore she did not necessarily experience this in the same way her older brothers and sister did, but she would have been there to witness some of the events and the spectacle of her siblings performing their duties.

It is through these court duties and events that the children would have had more contact with their parents, even if it was on a formal basis. The whole family were bonded by their duties as royals, and by their loyalty to one another and to their father's crown. It is perhaps at this point, as they grew older, that they became more conscious of their position and just what their future may look like. As they grew wiser to the world, their personalities would have been shaped to reflect the weight of their personal burden of expectations, and of the constant uncertainty and turmoil that came with their privileged positions.

Expectations were a theme throughout their education and their early years, learning manners and etiquette, learning languages to be better rulers and communicators, and becoming familiar with politics, history and even military tactics, to allow them all to be better prepared for what the future may hold. The king and queen were both conscious of how precarious their rule was, and the children would have been all too aware that this was their inheritance. For Arthur, the future fell on him more so than his siblings, but they all carried a burden. The girls would have wondered where they would be sent, and for what purpose. Henry, it could be argued, had the least weight to carry as his position as 'the spare' appeared to be less and less required as his brother took on his role as the Prince of Wales in the Marches and inched towards adulthood. His role as understudy came with its own issues however; his complete loyalty and the surrender of his personal freedom of choice was required in order to support the Tudor dynasty.

Chapter 6

Tragedy and Joy

While there had been political disruption and instability for Henry VII to deal with in the early years of his reign, probably the first time this directly affected the children – indeed the whole family – was in the autumn of 1495 when they suffered their first tragedy. Princess Elizabeth, the youngest of the Tudor children, passed away suddenly on 14 September, just after her third birthday.[1]

Her death appears to have been a shock and was certainly not expected as there are no records of doctors being called or any mention of ill health. Still, her death would have been a very sad event for a family who, up until this point, had seemed to have been so healthy and happy. Her parents were on progress in Northamptonshire, and a messenger was dispatched to tell them of her death, but they did not return at the news. The king ordered preparations for a grand funeral, and later he placed an order 'for diverse yards of silk bought for My Lord of York [Henry] and My Lady Margaret'.[2]

Elizabeth died at Eltham Palace where she and her siblings were spending their summer, and her body was placed in the chapel there for eleven days. Her infant body was covered with a cloth of pure gold thread, the Tudor coat of arms in the centre and displayed on boards all over the chapel. Candles were lit and incense burned while masses and requiems were sung for her.

After the eleven days in Eltham, a hearse drawn by six horses took Elizabeth, accompanied by her nurses, across the river to Westminster where the prior and monks of Westminster met the cortege to escort it to the Abbey. Elizabeth was placed in the choir of the Abbey, with a cloth of black velvet, fringed with red and white roses and lettered in gold *Jesus est amor meus*. The next day, the funeral service took place and mourners gathered to pay their respects to the little princess. She was given the grandest of funerals, the first of the dynasty, and almost a decade since her father had become king, her death shocked the nation.

After the services, her body was placed in a tomb in the Abbey. According to an 1853 guide to the Abbey she was placed originally in the chapel of St Edward the Confessor, and a memorial plaque was placed to her:

> Near that of Henry III. is a small monument in memory of Elizabeth Tudor, second daughter of Henry VII, who died at Eltham, in Kent, Sept. 14th, 1495, aged three years, from whence she was removed in great funeral pomp, and here buried.[3]

The plaque has since been lost, but records kept from the eighteenth century have it as saying:

> Elizabeth, second child of Henry the Seventh King of England, France and Ireland and of the most serene

> lady Queen Elizabeth his consort, who was born on the second day of the month of July in the year of Our Lord 1492, and died on the 14th day of the month of September in the year of Our Lord 1495, upon whose soul may God have mercy. Amen.[4]

There was also an effigy, which has also since been lost, which had a plaque. Again, records show it as reading:

> Hereafter Death has a royal offspring in this tomb viz. the young and noble Elizabeth daughter of that illustrious prince, Henry the Seventh, who swayed the sceptre of two kingdoms, Attrapos, the most severe messenger of Death, snatched her away but may she have eternal life in Heaven.[5]

If you visit the Abbey today, you can find a small chest, close to the tomb of Henry III, which once had these plaques attached to it.

As tragic as losing their youngest child may have been, the timing of this heartbreak could not have been worse for Henry and Elizabeth. Plots and problems with threats to their throne were of ongoing concern, and the position of England in Europe was in question as a result. Most counter-Tudor support was gathering around the pretender Perkin Warbeck, who claimed to be the younger of Edward IV's sons, Richard, Duke of York.[6] He had first come to light in 1490, and earlier in 1495 had even attempted to invade England, supported by

Margaret of Burgundy. While the invasion was unsuccessful, he had gained a lot of support in England and in other countries, including Scotland, where he had married Lady Catherine Gordon in 1496.

Around this time, negotiations began with Scotland to arrange the marriage of Princess Margaret to King James IV, and perhaps this was to provide an in-road for support against the Yorkist pretender. Margaret was just 6 years old when negotiations began, and it was normal for potential marriage treaties to be spoken of around this time. However, coming so close to such upheaval and after Princess Elizabeth's death, it may also have been an intention to secure their position while other things were causing turmoil.

In January 1495 King Henry had executed several of Warbeck's supporters, including Sir William Stanley who had supported Henry at the Battle of Bosworth and had been his Lord Chamberlain, for supporting Warbeck's claim and working against Henry to try to put the Yorkist pretender on the throne.

This political upheaval and danger to the dynasty was then compounded by diplomatic issues around the princess's death. Negotiations had begun for Elizabeth to be a potential bride to Charles of Castile, and now the treaty of which the marriage would have formed part, and which was of great importance to England's position in Europe, was under threat. The insecurity of the situation with Perkin Warbeck, and the unknown outcomes of treaties with major powers would have left England in a much less secure position and threatened to undermine the foundations of other alliances, such as the marriage of Prince Arthur to the Infanta Catherine.

However, by far the biggest impact was within the family themselves. Elizabeth was the youngest child, but she was 3 and an integral part of the family, the nursery, and the royal household. The four children meant that the family had lots to offer each other, and potential for the future, and now the family was incomplete again. All was not lost though; whether it was planned to add more children to the family, or whether it was a response to the insecurities that had occurred earlier in the year, by September 1495 and the death of Princess Elizabeth, the queen was pregnant once again.

Queen Elizabeth was 29 years old and was healthy and again, her pregnancy would appear to have gone smoothly. She went into her confinement at Sheen Palace, as she had done before, but perhaps there was more trepidation with this birth than there had been previously. While the pregnancy and the joy surrounding the arrival of a new baby was sure to have consoled both Elizabeth and King Henry, as well as the other siblings, it would have been a concern that Elizabeth was older, and the trauma of losing a child would very much have been front of her mind as the risk increased with every child, and every pregnancy.

On 18 March 1496, Elizabeth gave birth to a princess, whom she named Mary. The name Mary was popular generally in the period, and of significance to Elizabeth, who probably chose the name to honour her younger sister who had died in 1482, and with whom she was particularly close. However, following the loss of the Princess Elizabeth, there could also have been a religious influence in the decision to use the name. Prayer to the Virgin Mary was a common, daily practice, but Mary was also venerated by mothers and pregnant women, as well as those who were trying to conceive. The shrine to at Our Lady of Walsingham was a popular pilgrimage site, visited by Henry VII on his travels in 1487, and by Henry VIII and his first wife Queen Catherine of Aragon, during which Catherine made offerings and said prayers for the safe arrival of children for herself and her husband.[7] In 1502 Elizabeth's privy purse records that she sent an Easter offering to Our Lady at Walsingham alongside other pilgrimage sites, including Heyles Abbey, the site of the 'Holy Blood'.[8]

The birth of the princess was a relief to Henry and Elizabeth. As well as the safe arrival of another child and completion of childbirth for Elizabeth, another girl allowed them to once again reach out diplomatically to their allies with a potential marriage. It also meant that their little family had another baby to dote upon, which evidence suggests they really did. Records show that clothes for Mary were often elaborate, and descriptions include her wearing dresses of velvet, kirtles of satin and there is even an entry of her receiving fourteen pairs of double-soled shoes.[9] In 1504, when Mary was only 9 years old, Henry writes that he is providing his daughter with £100 a month as a personal allowance. This may have been a little exaggerated given the context, as Henry was writing to complain to King Ferdinand at his lack of support of his daughter, Catherine, who was living in London and having to be subsidised by Henry.

However, sums paid to Mary do appear in his spending records and as Maria Perry says, these sums and gifts were 'a generous allowance for a 9-year-old with no separate establishment and suggests that Mary was much cherished'.[10]

Mary would have joined the family nursery as an infant, just as her mother once again fell pregnant and this time, the baby was another boy. This was a great comfort to the family, as another male heir was much prized and after Princess Elizabeth's early death it is easy to imagine Henry and Elizabeth fearing for the lives of their remaining children. Their family was now larger and more secure, and the baby was welcomed by the king in particular.

The baby was named Edward, although some records show the name Edmund being used for him in some documents, which would have been significant for Henry, naming the child for his father, Edmund Tudor. He was born on 21 February 1499 at the Palace of Placentia, and this son and heir was baptised in splendour in the Church of the Observant Friars, just as his brother Henry had been.[11] Immediately his place was made secure in the family line of succession, and it was the king's intention to create him the Duke of Somerset.

By the time Prince Edward joined the nursery, the residents were Margaret, aged 10; Henry, aged 8; and Mary, aged 2 – and new arrival Edward, as well as Arthur, now 14 and set up well presiding over the Council of the Marches in Ludlow. Everything seemed to be going well for the family; for the younger children particularly, the older pair were able to take the younger children under their wings and, following the death of their sister, were probably very attached to their new baby brother and sister. Henry, who for such a long time had been the only boy in the household, now had a brother on whom he could rely, relieving the pressure on his status just a little, and he was no longer completely outnumbered in the nursery. Margaret and Mary would become close as they got older, with Margaret setting the example for her sister in what was expected of her as a Tudor princess. The children spent a great deal of time together, and when visitors came to see them at the palace, as happened in 1499 for the visit by Erasmus, all the children would have been present, including a 6-month-old Prince Edward. Together with the other children, such as Charles Brandon, the children took their lessons, they ate together and played together, and were a household.

Unfortunately, this happy little setup did not last long. In June 1500, Prince Edward died, aged just 15 months. At the time the children were at Hatfield House in Hertfordshire, where they had been sent to avoid an outbreak of plague in London. Sadly it seems likely that, due to the palace's large staff of people and the close connections it had with the city, the plague did reach the nursery at Hatfield, and this was probably the cause of Edward's premature death.[12]

The king and queen had been visiting the port of Calais in the month prior to his death, having sent the children out to keep them safe. They sailed back to England on 16 June 1500, and received news of the prince's death on the 19th when they were back on English shores. Again, they had been far away from their children when tragedy struck, and their youngest child was again the one that was taken from them. Upon their return to London the distraught parents arranged a funeral for their son at Westminster Abbey, and he was laid to rest with his sister, Elizabeth. Records show that the king and queen spared no expense, spending more than £240 on their son's funeral and his memorial in the Abbey, but unfortunately nothing of this has survived.[13]

Following the prince's death, a cloud of uncertainty was again cast over the court, and over the family. However, with four children who all appeared healthy, and a son about to reach adulthood, the family priorities could now switch from the lives of their young children, to securing the next generation of the monarchy. By early 1501, negotiations and preparations were in full swing for the imminent arrival of Princess Catherine, whom Arthur was to marry. All thoughts were focused on the fulfilment of an agreement that had first been decided when Prince Arthur was still a baby and that was meant to ensure that England, the Tudor dynasty, and the futures of each one of the Tudor children, would be remembered forever.

Chapter 7

The Children at Court

Edward's death in 1500 marks a change of pace in the situation at court and for the Tudor family. The royal family itself was once again in mourning for their lost sibling, and the king and queen had lost another child, an important son and heir. However, their surviving children were getting older and, except for Mary who was still only 5 years old, they were starting to emerge into the world of the court. Prince Arthur particularly was spending more and more time actively participating in decision-making at Ludlow and the Marches, taking responsibility for those lands, in preparation for his future role as king. He was attending meetings of the Council of the Marches and corresponding with his father and other nobles in his role as Prince of Wales.[1]

Princess Margaret and Prince Henry however, being based in and around London and in much closer contact with their parents and the court in general, started to play a more active role in court life. Perhaps this was a concerted effort to give them more experience and prepare them also for whatever role they may have in future, or perhaps it was an effort on King Henry's part to show the healthy Tudor family in their roles at court and front and centre so there could be no arguments about their claim or authority. In effect, the whole family were putting on a show to counteract any critics following the latest rounds of pretenders and threats to Henry's position on the throne.

Whatever the reasons, Prince Henry and Princess Margaret begin to feature more prominently at events and in court rolls. While they didn't have any roles to play due to their young ages, they appear to have taken on more ceremonial duties, supporting their parents at larger gatherings and representing them at smaller ones. Even younger sister Mary appears in some cases, observing her parents, brother and sister in their official duties, but not really taking an official role in proceedings. While we often see records of Margaret giving out prizes at tournaments, or representing her mother in church services, Mary is not mentioned.[2]

These appearances and duties performed by Margaret and Henry were similar to the ones that Elizabeth and her siblings, particularly her closest sisters, would have performed when they were coming up as princesses at the court of their father, Edward IV. They show that while the children were receiving a formal education and being kept apart from most of court life, they were also key members of the family, and ones that their parents would come to rely upon when more representation was needed. As royal parents Henry and Elizabeth would no doubt have been relieved that their children were now old enough to start commanding respect in their own right, and therefore to extend the reputation and influence of the family.

When Arthur began leading the Council of the Marches it was staffed by recommendations from his father, or from

Jasper Tudor. As time went on, however, Arthur became more familiar with the technical nature of ruling such an unstable area, and his opinions of those who worked with him and under him had more authority. Nobles vied to be close to Arthur and, despite the downsides of being in the relatively isolated Welsh borders, wanted to stay loyal, knowing that eventually he would succeed to the throne and their loyalty would potentially be greatly rewarded.

Domestically too, people tried to align themselves with the royal children, and those who were responsible for the children, especially as they got older and potentially started to gain power and influence. Although the relationship of the king and queen with their children was constrained by the royal protocols and the rigours of court schedules, they appear to have included family time together, and regular correspondence on both sides when their duties took them away; at these times, they were reliant on loyal nurses, tutors and family members to look out for the interests of the children.

Perhaps the person they turned to most was Henry's mother, Margaret Beaufort. Margaret may only have had one son, but she was a dedicated mother and an enthusiastic patron of the arts and education. She founded colleges at Cambridge university, built houses and sponsored poets and artists within her household at Collyweston, and she was devoted to her grandchildren.

She even left her own mark on the royal nursery palaces. At Eltham there were carvings of swans bearing her coat of arms, and she also held rooms at Sheen and at Placentia, particularly if Elizabeth was in confinement, so that she could be close and help when needed. When Henry and Elizabeth had first come to the throne of England, Margaret helped as best she could by arranging ceremonies and ensuring that all traditions were adhered to, underpinning her son's claim to the throne in the process.[3]

Lady Margaret, the Countess of Richmond, was particularly attached to her granddaughter Margaret, and took an interest in her from the very start, although this seems to have increased later when she was betrothed to the Scottish king and before she went to Scotland to take up her position as queen. Margaret seems to have been intent on protecting her family, especially her son and grandchildren, becoming an important and reliable support for both Henry and Elizabeth to lean on and a source of information they could utilise. In a similar vein, Elizabeth's mother and sisters were welcomed at court to support Elizabeth when she gave birth and while the children were young, recognising that the Tudor family were a large group, all working to support each other and achieve the best outcomes for the children.

By far the most important aspect of all the responsibilities held by everyone involved was to find their children suitable spouses. As royal children, whom they married, and when, was often – if not always – dictated by the needs of the king, and to improve the political standing of the country. Marriages would often form part of trade agreements, peace treaties, and other diplomatic interventions that were imposed on them by their parents and others in authority. All of Henry and Elizabeth's children would have known from a very young age that this expectation was placed upon them, and it was to be part of their royal duties to marry whoever was deemed fit and proper, and to do right by their parents, their spouses and by England.

To the same point, Henry VII and Elizabeth were approached by numerous European powers. While Margaret was probably destined for Scotland from quite early on, Mary's hand was highly sought after. The Duke of Milan wrote to Henry to see if she would be a potential bride for his son Massimiliano, Count of Pavia. This was turned down in favour of a renewal of the treaty and for Mary to be betrothed to Charles of Castile. However, this did not come to pass as he instead pledged to marry Louis XII's daughter Claude.[4] These approaches for marriage were almost always a diplomatic exercise, using the children to get something out of a relationship with England; the Duke of Milan hoped that Henry would ally with him in his disagreements with the king of France, but they could not come to terms. This could have been due to ongoing negotiations between the English crown and the Duke of Angoulême, who were talking of marriage between Prince Henry and the duke's daughter.[5]

Marriage was always the expectation and, as the eldest, the first of the children to take the plunge and marry was Prince Arthur. As we have already touched upon, from his earliest days it had been expected that Arthur would marry the Infanta, Catherine of Aragon, princess of Spain, as a part of the Treaty of Medina del Campo. While the intervening years had seen some aspects of the relationship between England and Spain changed, the aim of a marriage between England and Spain was always the central goal. In July 1496 Henry wrote to the Spanish royals to emphasise how it was 'very desirable that the alliance so long treated for should be concluded'.[6] The marriage was arranged and confirmed when Arthur and Catherine were considered old enough to be married, and so preparations began for the princess to come to England and a wedding to take place in the autumn of 1501.

Catherine left her home in Spain in August 1501, along with many escorts, ladies, her priests and other officials who would accompany her to make sure that everything went as smoothly as possible. There had already been delays to proceedings, as originally it was planned that she would travel to England in 1500. In the June of 1500, Henry VII had written to King Ferdinand, 'glad to have determined to send Catherine to England at the end of the summer'. However, just a month later he wrote again to say that he 'is willing to grant a delay until next summer', putting the wedding back to the summer of 1501 at the earliest.

The journey was fraught with issues from the very start. Originally departing on 17 August, the fleet was forced back to port by inclement weather which damaged the ships. King Henry sent his own joiners and craftsmen to assess the damage and help with repairs, as he did not want any further delays. The ships were supposed to arrive in England in Southampton in early October, but more bad weather sent the ships off course and the princess arrived on 2 October in Plymouth, Devon, almost 100 miles west of where she had been expected.[7]

Arrangements for the princess's arrival were hastily changed and officials were sent to greet her properly and welcome her to England.

Catherine travelled through the countryside, being greeted at every town and village by local officials and nobles, who would join the gathering crowd following the princess on her progress to London. She travelled through Devon and Dorset, and eventually up to the outskirts of the capital. There she was met by an even bigger group of nobles and officials, all acting on behalf of the king to greet her. Arrangements were made for her entrance into London to be spectacular and befitting the occasion and her status as a princess of Spain. In letters Henry ordered: 'that two litters be prepared for the said Princess's own person; one thereof to convey her by the way until she come to Croydon, the other to be more richly garnished that the first, to make her entry into London.'[8]

Before Catherine could get that far though, she was met with an unexpected request. King Henry had ridden out from London to meet her on her journey, having never met her in person he wanted to greet her, and for her to meet her future husband. Prince Arthur had travelled from Ludlow to be present in London when his bride arrived, so the royal parties travelled together to meet the princess at Dogmersfield, the home of the Bishop of Bath and Wells.[9]

This kind of meeting was unexpected, as under Spanish tradition Catherine would not necessarily have to see her husband before the wedding, let alone her father-in-law, but the Spanish party yielded to the king's request and they met on 6 November 1501. The princess had arrived at the house the night before and when the king and the prince arrived she was still in bed – probably exhausted from the long, arduous journey across a strange country, which had so far taken a month and she still had not reached her destination. The king insisted that he be seen by the princess immediately, even saying that he would see her while she was still in bed if necessary. This situation was truly unorthodox and must have been quite disturbing to 16-year-old Catherine – but if it was, she did not show it.

Prior to Catherine's arrival in England, at the request of either Queen Elizabeth or of Lady Margaret Beaufort, the Spanish ambassador wrote to request that Catherine and her ladies should learn languages: 'the future Princess of Wales should always speak French with her guest in order to learn the language and to be able to converse in it when she comes to England … This is necessary because the ladies do not understand Latin, much less Spanish.'[10] However, this advice does not appear to have been followed because during their meeting, Henry, Arthur and Catherine, had to communicate through translators or use their only common language – Latin.

During their first meeting, the king proclaimed that Arthur and Catherine should renew their vows of betrothal in person. Following a short ceremony, the king retired and left the party, and the betrothed couple were left alone for the first time. They spent some time dancing, and while the whole circumstance must have been awkward for them both, they could now see whom it was that they would spend their lives with.

Following the meeting, Arthur wrote to his future in-laws telling them how happy he was to have met his future wife, how beautiful she was, and generally expressing his happiness at their betrothal and marriage.[11] Although they had not previously met in person, the two had written to one another throughout their teen years, and we have drafts of letters sent by Arthur to Catherine. While their content isn't very enlightening, the fact that Arthur felt the need to draft letters before sending a finalised, neat copy to his future wife, shows the level of care and attention he gave their relationship even before they met.

The king also seems to have been impressed by Catherine herself. He wrote to her in most affectionate terms, offering her his support while she is in England:

> [Madam] I [beseech you that] it may please you to regard us hence forwards your good and [loving] father, as familiarly as you would do the King and Queen your parents, for on our part we are determined to treat, received, and favour you like our own daughter and in no wise more [or less dearly] than any of our own children.[12]

The following day Arthur returned to London, and Catherine and her group continued their progress towards the capital. She was headed towards Croydon, as originally planned, when she and her party were met on the road by a group of officials and the 10-year-old Prince Henry – the third member of her new family. They escorted the princess to Lambeth where she was expected by the Bishop of Rochester, and where she would stay for the next few nights while preparations were made for her grand entrance into the city.[13] On 12 November, a Friday, Catherine and her retinue entered the city, led by English nobles and Prince Henry, and made a journey through the streets taking in spectacular pageants, plays and other entertainments, all specifically designed to show how great England had become and how this marriage and alliance with Spain would make it greater still. Allegories on ancient history, mythology, biblical stories and even astrology all greeted the Spanish princess as crowds of thousands lined the streets to catch a glimpse of her as she passed through.

On Saturday 13th, the king and queen met with the gentlemen officials and with the Spanish ladies respectively. Henry laid on a spectacular show of force by lining the corridors of Baynard's castle with 300 yeoman guards and having a stage built for his newly commissioned throne to be placed upon. Queen Elizabeth arranged for a cortege of litters to transport the princess and her ladies to meet with her in person. After official matters were concluded, a less formal reception was held and the Spanish and English retinues all ate and drank to celebrate prior to the wedding which would take place the following day.

The wedding was probably the largest and most important occasion that any of the Tudor children had experienced in their lives. They all had roles to play, even the king and queen, and the whole event was designed to show England in the grandest light. Representatives from all over Europe were present, and

King Henry in particular was determined to put on the best show possible.

The ceremony took place in St Paul's Cathedral, and a stage and walkway were constructed for the couple to walk and stand on to say their vows, making them visible from anywhere in the cathedral. At about 9.30 am on Sunday, 14 November, Arthur took up his place at the altar to wait for his bride. A little while later Catherine entered through the west door, and she was escorted down the aisle by Prince Henry. She was followed by her ladies, and several English ladies also formed part of the bridal party, including Cecily of York, the queen's sister, who carried the princess's train.[14]

The bride and groom made an astonishing sight, dressed to match in white and cream, satin, lace, and velvet, and covered in jewels and pearls, and Arthur with his chains of office for the Prince of Wales; they would have looked spectacular on their stage, in the splendid surroundings of the cathedral which was covered in banners and tapestries, candles, gold and silver plate and painted walls, and stained glass taking in the morning light. The choir sang in jubilation, and the priests gave sermons and read passages about joyous beginnings and the return of the true Christ.

All of the children had roles to play in the wedding. Margaret and Mary would have been present, accompanying their mother and father to the ceremonies and to the receptions that followed. They would have received new clothing and been expected to represent England and themselves to the assembled dignitaries. All three would have watched in eager anticipation to see what would happen, and what was expected from their brother, to see what would eventually be expected of them in their own marriages.

Prince Henry took a more central role than his sisters, accompanying his sister-in-law to meet his brother at the altar, and was also dressed in all his finery, ready for the eyes of the entire assembled courts of Europe to be on him. This is something that perhaps he enjoyed; according to a poem by Erasmus dedicated to the 'invincible King Henry and on the exceptional character of his son', Henry's self-confidence was apparent. Maria Perry also states that Prince Henry, 'as second in line to the throne … had a very clear idea of his own importance'.[15]

Henry also made his mark at the reception that followed Arthur and Catherine's wedding, when all members of the court took part in dancing. Prince Arthur led out his aunt, Cecily of York, the king and queen danced together, and Prince Henry, 'having with him the Lady Margaret, his sister in hand came down and danced two bass dances'. This in itself isn't extraordinary, but what he did after did raise a few eyebrows: '[Prince Henry] perceiving himself encombered with his clothes, suddenly cast off his gown and danced in his jacket.'[16] Everyone appears to have loved Henry's extravagant performance, and this led to his exuberance appearing in a number of records of that day.

Throughout the celebrations, the elaborate staging and the entertainment, the main aim of the proceedings was to present the Tudor family as a united front and to show the clear line of succession from King Henry to his heir, Prince Arthur. The marriage between Arthur and Catherine carried the weight of expectation from both sides, and both the young people involved, while they probably enjoyed the frivolity and spectacle that was laid on to celebrate their union, must have felt like the weight of the world was on their shoulders. Perhaps Prince Henry could see that this was the case and in his own way was trying to support his brother and the rest of the family by bringing some laughter to the proceedings.

However, the newlyweds still had one more thing to get through before they could return to some sort of normality, and that was the wedding night. Following the ceremonies and celebrations, the bedding ceremony would be performed by members of the clergy and extended family. Even some members of the council might have been present to ensure that all was done correctly and that there could be no disputes later. Arthur would have been brought into the chamber where his bride, already in the bed, and helped by her ladies, would be waiting for him. Prayers would be said, and then the couple would be left to consummate the marriage. In some parts of Europe even this would be witnessed by the officials present, but for Arthur and Catherine, they were left alone.

This would prove controversial much later on, when Henry – by that time King Henry VIII – was trying to secure a divorce from Catherine; she was adamant that she and Arthur had not in fact consummated their marriage that night, or at any time during their marriage. She was insistent that she remained a virgin until her marriage to Henry a few years later, after

Arthur's untimely death. However, the morning after their wedding night, some of the men who were close to Arthur gave statements that the marriage had been consummated. Sir Anthony Willoughby, Arthur's companion for five years, said that the following morning the prince had emerged from the chamber announcing, 'bring me a cup of ale, for I have been this night in the midst of Spain', and then stating 'masters, it is a good pastime to have a wife'.[17] This display for his friends may have just been bravado on Arthur's part, or he could have been telling the truth and it was Catherine who was trying to preserve her dignity later on.

One other theory appears in some documents and may have been something that crossed people's minds at the time. A few years prior to the marriage of Arthur and Catherine, her brother Juan had died shortly after his marriage, and at a young age. The cause of death had been controversial and some thought that he had, in the words of Maria Perry, 'worn himself out through carnal excesses at an early age'.[18] While neither Arthur, nor Catherine, were considered young for marriage by their contemporaries, this recent loss of a young bridegroom may well have been on their minds, especially if there was any query about any weakness in his health. Were the young couple kept apart in those early weeks and months of their marriage so as to avoid any possibility of a repeat of the fate of young Juan?

Whatever the events or the reasons, we will never be sure what actually happened between the prince and princess on their wedding night or throughout their marriage, and this uncertainty is what contributed to what would come to be called Henry VIII's 'Great Matter'.

Following the wedding, and once all of the extended celebrations, jousts, banquets and masques had concluded, it was agreed that the royal couple would return to Ludlow, so Arthur could continue in his duties as Prince of Wales. The majority of Catherine's Spanish companions would return to Spain, taking with them gifts, documents and other royal patents to show that the marriage was now official. Catherine and a small number of her ladies remained in England, and would go to Ludlow, which was small and isolated in comparison to what they were used to in Spain, and even when compared to London. Catherine was also joined by some English ladies who would complete her household as the Princess of Wales, and she was left to get to know these relative strangers before they all travelled together to the Welsh Marches.

Catherine particularly was sad, and reticent for her Spanish companions, priests and other officials to go. She did not have a common language and would find communicating with her new husband difficult, and being so far removed from society made the move feel even more frightening for her. However, the king sweetened the deal, sending jewels for her and all her ladies as an icebreaker and to help her to feel welcome. By December 1501 she was resident at Ludlow and her ladies had formed a small court there, in some newly built apartments known as the Tudor lodgings. These mimicked the interiors of other palaces built and refurbished by the king at Richmond and Westminster, and would have been far more welcoming for the princess than the impression that the cold stone exterior of a medieval fortress would have given. In addition, the prince's other house at Bewdley also had improvements done to accommodate the new Princess of Wales and her ladies.[19]

The other children also went back to their normal business, but now there was added impetus to arrange weddings for them too. England had showed off her finery at the wedding of Arthur and Catherine, and the confirmation of the Spanish alliance gave England a more stable political position in wider Europe. Delegations were sent to speak to the French, the families connected with the Holy Roman Empire, to Scandinavia and, significantly for Margaret, to Scotland.

While negotiations had been ongoing for some time, they had somewhat stalled due to the Scottish involvement with Perkin Warbeck and their apparent support of his cause. The capture and execution of Warbeck and his supporters in 1499, and then the successful completion of the Spanish alliance and Arthur and Catherine's wedding in 1501 meant that now more than ever, an alliance with England was in Scotland's best interest.

Chapter 8

The Death of Arthur, Prince of Wales

The couple settled in quickly to their new roles at Ludlow. On their return there would have been more celebrations to introduce the new Princess of Wales to the local nobility that made up the Council of the Marches. While it was the middle of winter when they returned, people would have lined the streets when they passed through the local towns, hoping to see Catherine, Arthur's Spanish bride. The couple stayed on for Christmas and New Year in Ludlow, taking the opportunity to celebrate in a smaller way and get to know one another, and build relationships in their new households.

In a historical account of Ludlow Castle dating from 1754, their time at Ludlow was described: 'Arthur, Prince of Wales, eldest son of Henry VII, held a court of great splendour and magnificence here upon his marriage with Catherine of Aragon, a princess, say Historians, of such amiable and distinguished manners as rendered her an object of every one's admiration.'[1]

Christmas celebrations at court were lavish that year, as the court continued to play host to delegates who had attended the wedding but had been unable to make the crossings back to mainland Europe. The weather at that time of year made the crossing, even the short one from Dover to Calais, treacherous, and many stayed on or planned to return upon a break in the weather. As the New Year of 1502 began things looked hopeful for England and for the future of the Tudor Dynasty.

However, in the coming months a wave of illness, most likely the sweating sickness, swept across the country. The sweating sickness was catastrophic. Symptoms included dizziness, headaches and general malaise that would quickly turn into a burning fever, delirium and the extreme sweating that gave the illness its name. The physician John Caius, who was an English doctor who studied the disease during later outbreaks, concluded that death would normally occur between three and eighteen hours after the first onset of symptoms, but if the person was still alive after twenty-four hours, they would more than likely survive. Caius believed it to have been airborne, caused by the filth and lack of clean air in England's towns and cities, and while there have been theories regarding how the sickness began and how it spread, even today it is unclear what type of illness the sweating sickness was. What is known is that in years when the sweat hit, the mortality rate of those affected could be as high as 50 per cent. In one outbreak in 1485, the disease claimed approximately 15,000 lives in London alone.[2]

It was sometimes called the 'stop-gallant' because of how it affected young, otherwise healthy, gentlemen, but it was completely indiscriminate. If an outbreak happened, royals and nobility would take to their country houses to avoid the built-up cities where it appeared to thrive, but this was not always enough as it spread all the way across the country, and in the spring of 1502 the illness reached Ludlow.

Despite the efforts of doctors and officials to stem the tide of infections by closing Ludlow off to the outside world, it was too late. Both Arthur and Catherine were taken ill, and doctors were sent for. Their conditions were grave and, on 2 April 1502, Arthur died at just 15 years old. Catherine was still very poorly, so the news of his death was delayed until Catherine's condition was confirmed, and she was starting to recover.

His death was a shock to everyone. Some historians have queried whether Arthur had been a sickly child, perhaps due to being born a few weeks premature, or an underlying infection like tuberculosis which his father suffered from. However, there is no evidence to suggest that his death was in any way anticipated, or that he was suffering from any illnesses at the time of the wedding or afterwards.[3] This is what makes the sweating sickness, or another form of plague outbreak, the most likely cause of death.

As soon as Arthur's death was confirmed, officials had the task of telling his father, the king, what had happened to his eldest son. The messenger arrived at Greenwich on the evening of 4 April, and the king's councillors sent for his confessor, who was chosen to break the news to the king. Early on the morning of the 5th he entered the king's chambers and broke the news to Henry, whose first action was to send for the queen so that they 'wolde take the peyfull sorowes togyders'. When the queen arrived, she consoled the king, offering words of support and suggesting that their son had been chosen by God to leave them at such a young age, that their other children were all healthy and that they could still go on to have more children if God willed it. This seemed to help the king and soon the queen returned to her rooms where she became distraught, and this time the king came to her side to offer comfort to her.[4]

This type of display of emotion is unusual in accounts of royal events, and perhaps it gives us an insight into the relationship between Henry and Elizabeth, and also their love for their children. While Arthur was their eldest, and their heir, the fact that Elizabeth mentions their other children as consolation to Henry, perhaps helps them to see that the situation isn't completely disastrous. However, the more practical aspects are shown too, and the mention of having more children in order to bolster their position once more following the loss of Arthur shows their pragmatic side, their side that is focused on duty as well as personal feelings.

The parents were bereft, but so were the rest of the family. Margaret, Henry and Mary had all been centre stage at their brother's wedding just six months before, but now they were mourning his death. Prince Henry in particular saw an immediate change to his position as he was elevated by protocol to being the heir apparent to his father's crown. For Henry and Margaret, this was the third sibling they had lost in six years, and perhaps this fact was also the reason why Elizabeth was particularly stricken with grief. She ordered the whole court to be put into a state of mourning and ordered vast amounts of black clothing and fabrics for herself, her ladies, and her daughters.

Unfortunately, this was not the end of the sorry tale. Catherine, who had also been taken ill at the same time as her husband, was still very poorly. Once her recovery was assured however, then plans and preparations for Arthur's funeral were made. It is likely the delay in preparations was, to put things bluntly, to see if she recovered and ostensibly if they would need to plan a double funeral, or just one for Arthur. Once things were formalised, those around Arthur's household swung into action to plan his funeral and ensure that Catherine was taken care of appropriately.

It is likely that the funeral would originally have been arranged to take place in London, or at court, closer to the royal family. However, bad weather and poor roads in Shropshire and the rest of the Midlands stopped any transportation of Arthur's body back to London. Instead, his body was taken to Worcester Cathedral, travelling on an ox-cart due to the muddy conditions, and laid to rest in an elaborate ceremony organised by the bishops who could attend. His body was embalmed before burial and his internal organs removed and placed in a lead casket, which was buried in the chapel in Ludlow. One account tells us that this box was later to cause some controversy as it was removed, sold and then repurchased and returned to the chapel.

> Tradition informs us that the prince's bowels were deposited in the chancel of Ludlow church, and that his heart, contained in a leaden box, was taken up some time ago. This account, which has generally been disbelieved, seems to derive some credit from the following narrative, communicated through a channel of undoubted authority. On opening a grave in the chancel

> of Ludlow church some years ago a leaden box was discovered and sold by the gravedigger to one Robert Pitt, a plumber. This circumstance immediately coming to the knowledge of the then rector, Mr. Fenton, the box and its contents were repurchased and restored unopened to their former situation.[5]

Prior to the ceremony his body was placed in a wooden coffin and tightly wrapped in black waxed fabric to preserve it for transportation to Worcester. The coffin was placed in the audience chamber, surrounded by candles and on a plinth covered in gold cloth. He was attended by loyal residents of Ludlow, all of whom had received Maundy Thursday alms from him just a few weeks before his illness. They guarded him night and day until 23 April, three weeks after his death.

Worcester was chosen due to it being deep in the Marches, an area that Arthur knew well and to which he had deep connections, but this meant that none of his family were able to attend the funeral. Again, roads and isolation, bad weather and fear of the ensuing plagues and diseases that were making their way through the population meant that no one made the journey to Ludlow or to Worcester to see him buried. Despite this, the ceremony was lavish, and hundreds of mourners attended, from high-ranking nobles such as the Earl of Surrey, who was designated chief mourner, through to Arthur's nurse, Elizabeth Darcy, who had taken care of him at Farnham.[6]

In preparation for the funeral six horse-drawn carts loaded with fabric were sent from London to make mourning clothes for those who were to attend. Banners were made by the king's court painters to accompany the prince's body on its journey, and then again during the funeral itself. Arms of the king and queen, prince and princess, alongside those of the king and queen of Spain. Flags with the crests of Cornwall, Chester, and of the ancient heraldic legacies of Cadwallader and Brutus, were all painted and put on display in Worcester Cathedral, carried in as part of the funeral processions, first through Ludlow and then on to Worcester.

On 23 April Arthur's body was taken to the church in Ludlow for the first of his public funeral services, and all of the symbols and imagery that had followed Arthur throughout his life, carried on into his funerary offerings and followed his body as it travelled from Ludlow to Worcester for his second service in the cathedral on 25 April. Historian Johan Huizings points out: '[Such festivals] still preserved something of the meaning they have in primitive societies, that of the supreme expression of their culture, the highest mode of collective enjoyment and as assertion of solidarity.'[7]

In the absence of any members of the royal family, the funeral of Arthur needed to link the Welsh Marches and the crown; to ensure that their authority and the loyalty that Arthur commanded continued despite his death. Imagery from the past was paired with that of the future of the Tudor dynasty, demonstrating that the line remained intact.

As the mourners assembled at the cathedral, both inside and out, a chair was put out for Catherine, but she did not attend. It may have been that because no other members of the royal household were there, protocol would have prevented her from attending on her own. Or, she may still not have been well enough to travel to Worcester to attend the ceremonies in their entirety. Whatever the circumstances, it was left to the Earl of Surrey, to complete the services and oversee the most elaborate funeral that Worcester Cathedral had ever seen. Just six months after England had, in great pomp and ceremony, seen its first heir to the throne married in nearly a century, he was buried far from his family and home.

Following his funeral ceremony, an elaborate tomb was constructed by order of the king. The stone sarcophagus which would hold his body was covered in symbols of Arthur's rank, his royal lineage, and his status as Prince of Wales. He is surrounded by Tudor images, portcullises from his grandmother's Beaufort line, and other heraldic symbols. The imposing shrine that surrounds the tomb itself was designed to impose a presence over the whole cathedral. While the king and queen did not travel to see their son buried, they worked to ensure that this legacy continued in the Marches, even after his death. They intended to show how much potential he had held, and to capitalise on the loyalty he had commanded to shore up their own position in the region.

Despite all of these intentional actions by the royal family and their loyal nobles, as soon as the funeral was over, Arthur's household was disbanded and King Henry and the whole of England, had to adapt to the new circumstances that faced them. The title of Prince of Wales now passed to Prince Henry who was almost 11 years old at the time of his brother's death. Plans were made for him to take up his brother's mantle and in June 1502, only a few of months after Arthur's death, negotiations began between England and Spain for Henry to marry his brother's widow, Princess Catherine, to maintain their alliance. Although it took a long time due to the papal dispensations that would be required for them to marry, a treaty was signed in June 1503, and plans put in place that Henry and Catherine would marry on 28 June 1505, Prince Henry's fifteenth birthday.

His education and position in the royal nursery were continued, with some idea that he would soon take his brother's place in Ludlow, heading up the Council of the Marches, in preparation for when he would become king. For the princesses, they faced the loss of another sibling, not this time to an unforeseen death, but their brother, with whom they had spent their entire young lives, was to be taken from them to live in the Midlands, and there was always the prospect that they may never see him again. While they had not been particularly close to Arthur, he would have been a presence in their lives in the same way that their parents were, and his loss would have served as a reminder of their own mortality, and of the fragility of their own positions.

For Margaret though, the shock was perhaps the greatest. Immediately after Arthur's wedding in November 1501 negotiations had been gathering pace between England and Scotland, arranging for her own wedding to the king of Scotland. In January 1502 a marriage treaty known as the Treaty of Perpetual Peace was finally signed by the two kings and a proxy marriage ceremony had taken place at the brand new Richmond Palace, attended by the king and queen and their children. The treaty also included restrictions on the movement of 'rebellious subject', and that anyone moving between the two nations would require letters of introduction from the king to enter without suspicion, put in as protection from either party harbouring challengers to the throne or traitors, as the Scots had done with Perkin Warbeck.

The ceremony was overseen by the papal representative as well as three archbishops and four bishops, such was the importance of the event. The Earl of Bothwell acted as the representative of King James of Scotland. According to Polydore Vergil:

> At about this time James, King of Scotland, sent an embassy to King Henry to seek his daughter in marriage. Henry received the embassy with great kindness. He did not reject the requests of James and betrothed to him his twelve-year-old daughter, Margaret, so that by this marriage alliance friendly relations should for ever be cemented.[8]

At the ceremony itself, promises were made, that the King of Scots would 'for her all others forsake', and the princess spoke solemn vows in return:

> I, Margaret, the first begotten daughter of the right excellent, right high and mighty Prince and Princess, Henry by the grace of God, King of England and

> Elizabeth, Queen of the same, wittingly and of deliberate mind having twelve years complete in age in the month of November last past, contract matrimony with the right high and mighty Prince, James, King of Scotland until and for my husband and spouse and all other for him forsake.[9]

From that point Margaret was referred to in documents and ceremonies as 'Queen of Scotland', and was placed ahead of her siblings, and treated with equal standing as her mother in most cases. At the reception that followed the proxy wedding ceremony Elizabeth took her daughter by the hand and escorted her to the queen's dining table, where they ate together. Prince Henry, on the other hand, was not so happy about his sister's elevation, and one story tells that when he realised his sister was now a queen rather than a princess, he was so angry that he cried and refused to acknowledge her.

To celebrate the marriage alliance parties and jousts were held, and Margaret gave out the prizes to the winners on the tiltyard, and celebrations went on for days afterwards. However, not everyone was happy about the alliance with Scotland and some of the king's councillors pointed out that future heirs to the Scottish throne produced by Margaret and King James, would in fact have a claim to the English throne also, which they viewed as potentially problematic. Henry dismissed the idea:

> Supposing, which God forbid, that all my male progeny should become extinct, and the kingdom devolve by law

> to Margaret's heirs, will England be damaged thereby, or rather benefited? For since the less becomes subservient to the greater, the accession will be that of Scotland to England, not of England to Scotland.

He added descriptively that Scotland would be added to England 'as a rivulet to a fountain'.[10]

Following Arthurs's death, it was only Margaret's marriage to Scotland which appeared as a bright light on the horizon, as the alliance with Spain hung in the balance. Princess Catherine was still living in Ludlow until a time after Arthur's death, recovering from her own illness and mourning the loss of her husband. However, in the summer of 1502 she moved, along with her ladies, back to London, and was given an allowance by Henry VII until her circumstances became clearer. The king and the Spanish had a contract of marriage, and Henry was duty bound to complete this, mainly due to the financial benefits to the crown. Catherine's dowry, the money that her family were expected to pay to England, was substantial, and Henry had already earmarked large portions of it to projects, and to Princess Margaret's dowry and household to send to Scotland. However, Prince Henry was only 11, and too young to marry, especially to a bride who was significantly older than him. Catherine was effectively left in diplomatic limbo while her father and King Henry came to arrangements about her future.

Catherine's household also came under Queen Elizabeth's favour and she would often sent gifts or help her with daily purchases. According to Elizabeth's privy purse accounts she gave Catherine use of her barge with sixteen rowers (there would be twenty if the queen was using the barge) and, on another occasion, she paid 10 shillings for a package of books to be sent to her.[11]

While she remained in England, however, her father did have some use for her, as he made her the official ambassador to the English court. This gave her opportunities to be seen by King Henry, and to perhaps exert some influence on her own situation, while also giving her a role and a purpose while she remained in England. While she was there she, as the Dowager Princess of Wales, and her ladies gained a reputation as benefactors of the arts and as a group of well-educated women. Catherine had been educated at her mother's court, starting at the age of 4 in classical Latin and the study of the scriptures, and it was Isabella's influence that led Catherine to carry on in similar pursuits. She invited artists from Spain and Italy to come to stay with her, and she brought European fashions, music and literature that the courtiers in London had never seen before.

Catherine's influence during this period can be seen in the work of Pietro Torrigiano, a Florentine artist who had been forced to flee Italy after he broke Michelangelo's nose in a fight.[12] He was invited to England in the early 1500s and commissioned by Henry VII, and subsequently by a young Henry VIII to create Henry VII's tomb at Westminster Abbey. It is likely that he was known to Catherine and her family through their connections on the Continent and to other artists, and this is how his work came to be known in England.

The dowager princess's house also welcomed Princess Mary as a regular visitor. She had been somewhat left behind by the events that had caused her nursery companions to leave her side, and in 1502, at the age of 6, she was now starting on her formal education. In just the same way as her siblings, Mary was aware from an early age that she was to marry for diplomatic purposes. Alliances with the French and with the Spanish were considered for her, a French maid was employed for her to practice French conversation with, and it could be that her tutors and mistresses thought that being in the presence of Catherine and her ladies, and learning from them would be beneficial for her.

Despite all of the grief and disruption caused by Arthur's death, the family appeared to be pulling together and taking stock of what they could use to their advantage. The whole Tudor ship had been rocked and now it needed to be steadied. Henry and Elizabeth set to work in ways that had succeeded so well before; Henry by concentrating on negotiations for the other children's marriages, on foreign alliances and settling issues of the succession, and quashing political threats domestically as further opposition claimants to his throne continued to try to depose him. Possibly the best news of all for Henry though was that Elizabeth was pregnant once again.

Chapter 9

The Death of a Queen

Elizabeth's pregnancy was good news after a slew of bad. Maybe the statement that the queen made about them still being young enough to have more children immediately after Arthur's death was being put to the test, or it was a result of the king and queen turning to each other for comfort in this time of grief. Whatever the circumstances, by the autumn her pregnancy would have been confirmed with the baby expected to arrive in the early spring of 1503. One charming entry in Elizabeth's accounts in the winter of 1502 includes an entry which reads: 'To mistress Belknap for a reqard given to a servant of Bishop Rochester for bringing a present of grapes to the Queene – 3s 4d.'[1]

It is possible that Elizabeth was craving grapes, and the servant who had been able to procure some, in the middle of winter, had been handsomely rewarded.

However, this pregnancy was not without risks, and everyone involved in the royal household would have been very aware of those risks. They had already lost two children in infancy and Elizabeth was now 36 years old, which even today would be considered a higher risk pregnancy. Childbirth was already considered a dangerous thing for a woman to go through, with risks of complications and infections being extremely high.

Recent studies have concluded that maternal mortality rates due to problems in childbirth itself was as high as twenty or even thirty deaths per thousand births.[2] Elizabeth's history of childbirth was, however, promisingly problem free, so no one in the household foresaw any issues with this pregnancy or birth.

Confinement preparations were now a well-oiled machine for Henry and Elizabeth, and they knew exactly what was expected of them both. This time, Elizabeth's confinement was arranged to take place at Richmond, and new plush furniture was ordered to redecorate the queen's apartments there. A new bed with curtains, embroidered with clouds, flowers and Tudor Roses, was commissioned ready for the birth, and everything was made ready for the new arrival.[3]

However, the plans that had been made did not come to fruition. On 2 February the king and queen were at the Tower of London taking part in celebrations for Candlemas Day. Later that day the queen 'travailed of child suddenly' and went into labour earlier than expected. She would have taken to her chambers at the Tower, accompanied by her midwife, Alice Massey, and her ladies of her household. It is likely that Princess Margaret played a role in proceedings, as Elizabeth's eldest daughter and as queen of Scotland in preparation for her own marriage, it would have been a support for Elizabeth to have her daughter present for the birth. It would have been a good learning experience for Margaret, allowing her to see how she would need to prepare, to behave and what to expect physically.

Late on 2 February 1503, Elizabeth delivered a baby girl whom they named Katherine. The name was again a traditional choice, naming the child for one of Elizabeth's siblings and, also, the newest member of the court, Princess Catherine. The Dowager Princess of Wales had endeared herself to the queen enough for this to be a consideration. For all the good intentions of naming the baby so thoughtfully, unlike for her older siblings a simple baptism was held 'upon the Saturday after … within the parish church of the Tower'.[4] This private baptism may be explained by the baby's premature arrival and concern that the baby was in poor condition at birth. On 8 February the king ordered cushions and blankets for the baby's cradle, and put in place nurses and rockers for her, but neither the child nor her mother had left the confines of the Tower.

Just a day after preparations had begun for Katherine's personal household to take shape, Elizabeth became desperately ill. This time her experience of childbirth had not gone smoothly and it had taken its toll on her physically. She remained in her bed after the baby was born, hoping to rest and recuperate but to no avail. On 10 February Elizabeth's illness progressed and that evening doctors were summoned to her bedside. This effort was to no avail; on the morning of the 11th, Elizabeth of York, 'the most virtuous princess and gracious Queen', died.[5] It would have been her thirty-seventh birthday.

The closeness of her death to the birth of Princess Katherine would suggest that Elizabeth was taken by 'childbed fever' or puerperal fever. This is the same thing that would, years later, take Jane Seymour following the birth of Prince Edward, the future King Edward VI; for Jane, it had begun following a difficult birth which had probably caused an infection from which she never recovered. It was common for women to succumb to this type of infection due to the lack of hygiene and knowledge and as a result the symptoms of childbed fever were well known: high fevers, headaches, dizziness and lesions in the skin. Without modern medicine and antibiotics it was not possible to treat and almost always led to the death of the mother. If a woman was exhausted by a long labour, perhaps lost a lot of blood, and had not been able to give birth in a clean and calm environment, the risk of this type of illness were greatly increased.

As soon as it became clear that the queen would not recover, the king and her attendants would have called for a priest to administer the last rights. Henry would have stayed with her until the very end, and his grief was well documented. As he was not to attend her funeral, he gave the responsibilities for the arrangements for the ceremonies to the Earl of Surrey, who had arranged Arthur's funeral also. He headed for Richmond to be in solitude:

> [The queen's] departing was as heavy and dolorous to the King as ever was seen or heard of, and likewise to all estates of his realm, as well citizens as commons, for she was one of the most gracious and best beloved princesses in the world in her time being….
>
> …took with him certain of his secretest, and privily departed to a solitary place to pass his sorrow and would that no man should resort to him but such as his Grace appointed.[6]

While the king mourned, he left all the arrangements for the funeral and for running his household to his mother, Lady Margaret Beaufort. She had always been something of the matriarch of the family, but now she had to step up to help her son, and the rest of his family, to navigate the aftermath of a period of time that could be considered their very own *annus horribilis*.

In three years, the king had lost two of his sons, including his almost adult heir, his wife, and the loss of Princess Elizabeth prior to that had also added to the compounding of grief and stress that fell upon him. He was also aging – at the time of Elizabeth's death was 46 years old, and had led a hard life in exile which made him look older than his years. His health was failing, and he was showing signs of tuberculosis which became worse every year and took him longer each time to recover from bouts of coughing and illness.

Politically the situation in England was still far from calm, and threats from families such as the de la Poles continued to cause issue with him both at home and abroad. They claimed to be the true heirs to the English throne through their claim to the Dukedom of Suffolk. John de la Pole had died at the Battle of Stoke in 1487, but his younger brother Edmund was not loyal to Henry VII, eventually fleeing to Europe in 1501, where he was harboured by the Holy Roman Emperor as a part of negotiations for alliances. It wasn't until 1506 that Henry managed to negotiate Edmund's handover to England. Edmund was then put in the Tower until eventually he was executed in 1513 by Henry VIII, having once again tried to threaten the king's position. In 1503, however, he was still at large in Europe and able to garner support at the English court, he represented a major threat to Henry's control of England.

Henry's departure from the Tower and absence from court indicates just how upset he was by his wife's death. A king would not normally be able, let alone want, to isolate himself in such a way, but perhaps it was because he had lost his supportive wife, and that his new-born daughter was possibly born poorly, that the king did not want to interact with the day-to-day life of the court where they had made their life together.

On 18 February (although it may have been a few days earlier than this as records are incomplete), just days after Elizabeth's death, their new-born daughter, Katherine, also died. Princess Katherine was taken and buried in Westminster Abbey, most probably with her sister and brother, close to the tomb of Edward the Confessor. While previously the children had been given funerals and commemorations, the court's full attention centered on the funeral of Queen Elizabeth, and her funeral was to be the grandest that London had seen for a long time.

Preparations began almost immediately, and within a day Elizabeth's body was dressed in state robes so that her children could come to visit her and say their goodbyes. All of the children were provided with new mourning clothes so that they were properly attired for the period of mourning. Elizabeth's household accounts show that they already had clothes for the mourning period for Arthur, but still more were required for the loss of their mother and queen. Once this was done, the body was cased first in wax, then lead, then in a casket of holly wood, then the coffin was wrapped in black velvet and damask, similar to the way Arthur's coffin was wrapped less than a year before.[7] The coffin was taken to the chapel of St Peter ad Vincula within the Tower, where, surrounded by candles and with its highly decorated walls draped with black, she lay in state for eleven days.

Poetry and elegies to the queen were put up on boards for those who were to come and pay their respects while she lay in state. One poem was written by a young lawyer who would go on to be very well known at the court, Sir Thomas More:

'A Rueful Lamentation on the Death of Queen Elizabeth'

O ye that put your trust and confidence,
In worldly joy and frail prosperity,
That so live here as ye should never hence,
Remember death and look here upon me.
Example, I think, there may no better be.
Yourself know well that in this realm was I,
Your queen but late, and lo
now here I lie.

Was I not born of old worthy lineage?
Was not my mother queen, my father king?
Was I not a king's wife in marriage?
Had I not plenty of every pleasant thing?
Merciful God this is a strange reckoning:
Riches, honor, wealth, and ancestry
Hath me forsaken and, lo now, here I lie.

The poem carries on, naming each individual member of the family and presenting Elizabeth as a loving mother and wife. Interestingly, the references to Katherine in the later verses refer to her as still living, suggesting that this poem was written hastily within a couple of days of Elizabeth's death:

Adieu, mine own dear spouse, my worthy lord,
The faithful love that did us both combine,
In marriage and peaceable concord,
Into your hands here I clean resign,
To be bestowed upon your children and mine.
Before were you father, and now must ye supply,
The mother's part also, for lo now here I lie.

Farewell, my daughter, lady Margaret;
God knows how often it has grieved my mind,
That ye should go where we should seldom meet.
Now am I gone, and have left you behind.
O mortal folk, that we be very blind,
That we least fear, how often it is most near,
From you depart I first, and lo now here I lie.

Farewell, Madam, my lord's worthy mother,
Comfort your son, and be ye of good cheer.
Take all a worth, for it will be no other.
Farewell, my daughter Katherine, late the wife
To prince Arthur, mine own child so dear
It remedies not for me to weep and cry;
Pray for my soul, for now lo here I lie.

Above: Portrait of Henry VII & Elizabeth of York.

Right: Winchester Round table, showing the Tudor Rose in the centre.

An artist's rendition of Richmond Palace on the banks of the River Thames, 1638, by Wenceslaus Hollar.

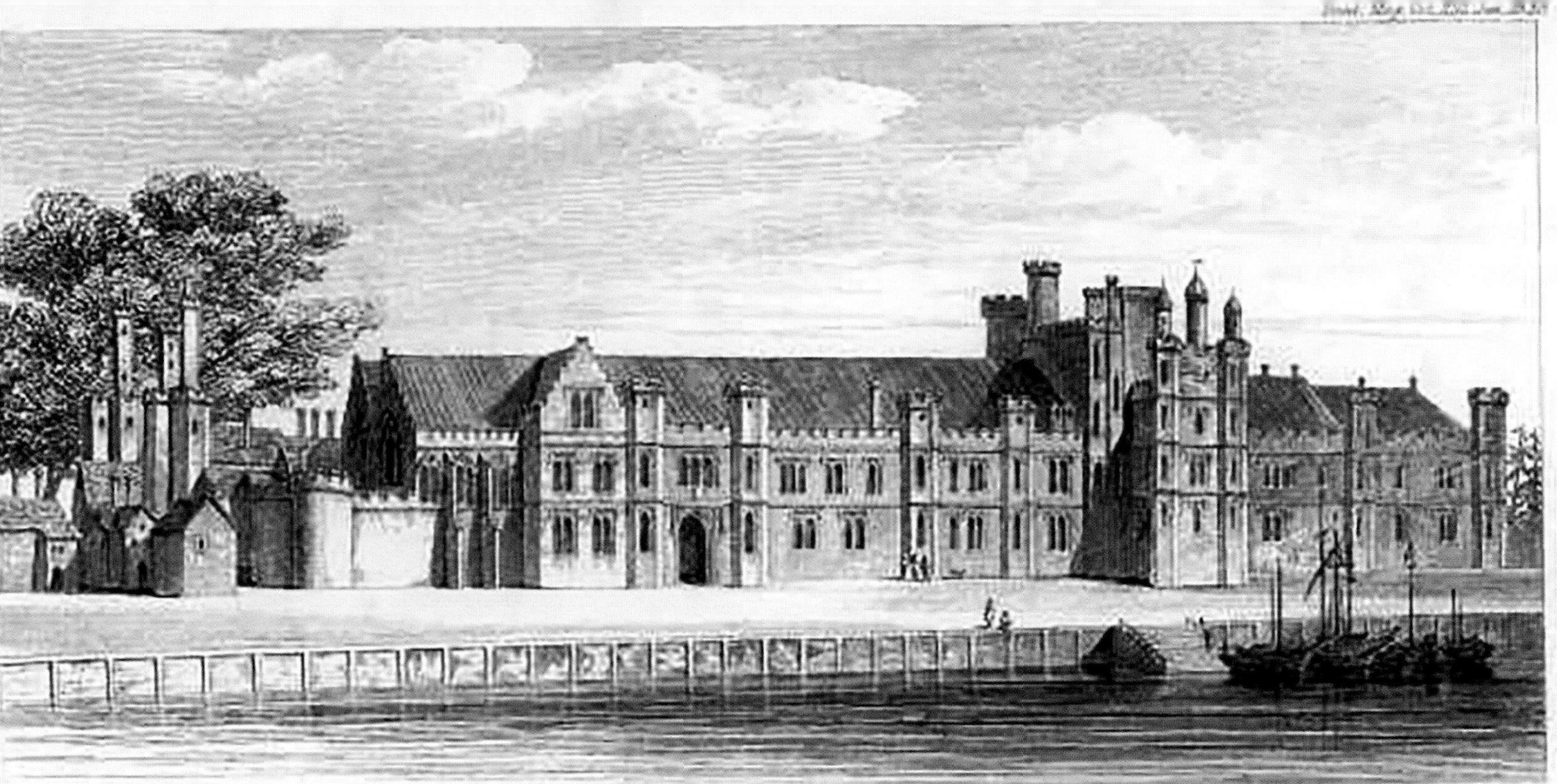

Greenwich Palace.

A passional, showing Henry VII at the time of the death of Elizabeth of York, and their surviving children.

Prince Arthur, by Harry John Wilmot-Buxton.

Prince Henry, by Harry John Wilmot-Buxton.

Copy of a contemporary portrait of Margaret from the Recueil d'Arras.

Plaque on 'Queen Margaret's Arch' in York. (Author's own)

'Queen Margaret's Arch' in York. (Author's own)

Copy of the Whitehall Mural. King Henry VIII and Jane Seymour, King Henry VII and his wife Elizabeth of York. Engraving by G. Vertue after R. van Leemput after H. Holbein. (Wellcome Collection)

Adieu, Lord Henry, my loving son, Adieu.
Our Lord increase your honour and estate;
Adieu, my daughter Mary, bright of hue.
God make you virtuous, wise, and fortunate.
Adieu, sweet heart, my little daughter Kate;
Thou shalt, sweet babe, such is thy destiny,
Thy mother never know, for lo now here I lie.[8]

The poem, and others like it which were displayed and reproduced throughout England after her death, show how much Elizabeth was loved, and how revered she was by the people. It also gives some voice to how her children felt about her. Although Thomas More would not have been privy to how the family was feeling about the death of their wife and mother, we do have some evidence to suggest that his words were, at least in some small way, accurate.

One such piece of evidence is an image taken from an illuminated manuscript produced shortly after Elizabeth's death, which shows the family and their responses to her passing. In the image, which is now in the archives of the National Library of Wales, we can see the king on his throne and receiving his councillors.[9] However, behind him in what could be any family home, we see two young girls sat on the floor sewing or weaving, and in the background we see a figure of a young boy slumped over the end of a bed. The two girls represent the Princesses Margaret and Mary, taking to their feminine work and happy in each other's company, in front of a roaring fire, secure behind their father's throne. The boy however, is obviously distraught, with his head in his arms.

This boy is Prince Henry. He is alone, having lost his mother and his older brother, and is the representation of the family's grief, as well as their now precarious future.

The image is part of a book which was presented to the king as a gift and would have been highly valuable at the time, but that this image is included suggests that the family's turbulent times were well known to those around them, and that the grief they felt was both accepted and shared by others.

Another way we can tell just how distressed the family were at Elizabeth's passing, especially King Henry, is by the extravagance of her funeral and the ceremonies and memorials performed all over England. Immediately after her death, sermons and prayers were said for her all over England, and candles were sent to shrines such as Our Lady at Walsingham, so that they may be lit in her memory. This continued throughout the eleven days that she lay in state at the Tower. On 22 February her coffin was moved through the streets of London to Westminster Abbey, covered in fringed velvet drapes and pulled by six horses draped in black velvet also. Every church they passed on the route was also draped in black shrouds and their bells tolled as she passed.[10]

Throughout, no expense was spared and the whole event cost over £2,800, which equates to almost £1.5 million if the same were spent today. This contrasts starkly with Henry's reputation as a miser who refused to spend money, and perhaps gives us yet another indication of the affection and respect that was felt by the king towards his wife, and what he felt he had lost in her passing. The funeral itself encompassed two days of masses and ceremonies, and involved hundreds of people including all of Elizabeth's surviving relatives who came to pay their respects. Conspicuous by their absence though were the king and the prince and princesses, all of whom remained in seclusion, mourning their loss and grieving together.

For Prince Henry, the loss of his mother was a major blow. The depiction of him crying, kneeling at the foot of a bed that could very well have been his mother's, paints a picture of a child who had his entire world turned upside down, and in a little over a year he had gone from the boy who danced vivaciously at his brother's wedding, to the motherless child-heir to the throne of England, with very little warning or preparation.

However, it could be argued that his sisters' experiences of the loss were keener. Princess Mary was still only 6 years old and had lost brothers and sisters and now her mother, without ever really getting to know any of them. While she was praised for her beauty and her charming nature by all who came into contact with her, her young age and the compound effect of the losses of family members would have taken its toll on her. Margaret was older, and understood how impactful her mother's death was on everyone, not least the political and diplomatic issues that threatened their positions now and in the future. She would also have been keenly aware of her own impending journey and change in circumstances to being queen of Scotland, something that she would have wanted her mother's support in navigating. In the months prior to Elizabeth's death, she had spent a lot of time with Margaret, teaching her how to deal with diplomats and her subjects, and helping her to adjust to life as a queen. They had gone everywhere together and her expenses show that Elizabeth generously provided all of the resources that a queen should have, including exquisite clothing, books and other things to take with her to Scotland, including household items. On 8 June 1502 Elizabeth's privy purse accounts show: 'to Henry Roper, for stuf by him bought for the Quene of Scottes; Pewter basins, washing bowles, a pair of bellows – 11s 10d.'[11]

Losing her mother at such an important point in her life would have been a massive blow to the young Margaret, who would now have to remember all her mother had taught her, and rely instead on her grandmother and other ladies at court.

All the children also had to maintain their composure while dealing with court proceedings in this period of mourning. Even Princess Mary would be expected to wear mourning clothes and attend church services and special occasions such as religious holy days, all while still trying to grieve for their mother. The king chose to engross himself in his work and his duty to his country, while remaining at Richmond in seclusion for months following his wife's death; this meant that court life and ceremonies fell on the children, particularly Margaret and Henry, to keep up with the normal calendar of events which would usually be performed by the king and queen.

King Henry did, however, focus on trying to ensure that, despite all the losses and struggles that the family had endured in 1502–1503, the future was brighter for them and for the whole country. In this vein, marriage arrangements for Margaret moved on apace. Her betrothal to the king of Scotland and her position as the future queen meant that she, at the tender age of 14, was the most senior royal woman at court. However, the king now had to make sure that her marriage went ahead and the Treaty of Perpetual Peace would come to fruition.

Margaret's preparation began when she was sent to live with her grandmother, Margaret Beaufort, at her home of Collyweston, north of London. This would have been for several reasons, but as Margaret's mother was no longer around to prepare her, it would have fallen to Margaret Beaufort to ensure that the young princess was ready for the journey to Scotland and ready for all of the duties that her marriage would entail.

It may well have been Lady Margaret Beaufort's influence that meant that the princess was kept in England as long as she was. Lady Margaret had given birth to her only son, the king, when she was only 13 and never had another child, despite being married more than once. A birth at 13 could well have caused her an enormous amount of trauma, both physically and mentally, and this experience would probably have made her very protective of her young granddaughter who, in much the same way, was to be married to an older, more experienced man. However, after Elizabeth's death, diplomacy became more important than any physical wellbeing concerns for the young girl, and so arrangements were made for her to travel to Scotland in the summer of 1503. On 27 June, just four months after Elizabeth was buried, it is recorded that Henry left Richmond to travel with Princess Margaret to Collyweston and bid her farewell on her journey to Scotland.

They did not travel alone. An entry in Lady Margaret's book of hours describes that on 5 July, 'This day 1503 King Henry VII and the Queen of Scots, his daughter will a great multitude of lords and other noble persons came to Collyweston unto my Lady his mother.'[12]

They stayed at Collyweston for up to three weeks before setting out on the month-long journey to Edinburgh. The king returned to London and left his daughter in the care of the Earl of Surrey and his wife; Henry even sent John Yonge as chronicler to keep a record of what occurred on the journey and at the wedding.

With Margaret's departure, and with the king still keeping to his rooms at Richmond most of the time, Prince Henry and Princess Mary were left as the only two in the royal nurseries. What had once been a lively and happy household full of children and laughter, now became a serious place of purpose and preparation for future roles of the two young people. Henry turned 12 just before Margaret left, and this meant that all eyes were now on him as the heir to the throne and as Henry's only hope for a Tudor dynasty. Mary was still only small, but she could not help but see how things had changed over the past few years and months, and how these changes would have serious consequences for her, her family and for England.

Chapter 10

The Later Reign of Henry VII

In the summer of 1503, the Tudor court was a quiet place. The king had become a solitary creature, focusing on the security of his realm and his legacy as king. His main aim was ensuring that he passed on his throne to his heirs, and he was determined to do it. From Polydore Vergil we get a clear idea of what Henry was like at this time, as he wrote about him in his 1513 *Historia Anglica*:

> His body was slender, but well built and strong; his height above the average. His appearance was remarkably attractive and his face was cheerful, especially when speaking; his eyes were small and blue, his teeth few, poor and blackish; his hair was thin and white; his complexion sallow.
>
> His spirit was distinguished, wise and prudent; his mind was brave and resolute, and never, even at moments of greater danger, deserted him. He had a most pertinacious memory; he was not devoid of scholarship.
>
> In government, he was shrewd and prudent, so that no one dared to get the better of him through deceit or

> guile. He was gracious and kind and was as attentive to his visitors as he was easy of access. His hospitality was splendidly generous; he was fond of having foreigners at his court. But those of his subjects who were generous only with promises he treated with harsh severity.
>
> He was most fortunate in war, although he was more inclined to peace. He cherished justice above all things. He was the most ardent supporter of our faith and daily participated with great piety in religious services, but all these virtues were obscured latterly by avarice. In a monarch indeed it may be considered the worst vice, since it is harmful to everyone.[1]

It was also at this time that Henry decided it was time he found himself another wife. With only one male heir, his legacy and the Tudor dynasty was far from secure and the only way to make it secure was to form another alliance, marry again, and make another heir or two. To attract another wife Henry commissioned a number of portraits of himself which could be distributed and viewed by any potential brides. The portraits, one of which is now in the National Portrait Gallery, shows an older Henry, very similar in looks to his funeral effigy which also survives, dressed in fine clothes and holding a red rose.

The portrait was sent all over Europe in the hope of securing a new wife and this became something of a preoccupation for him. Potential wives from France, Spain and Italy were courted, but none came forward offering marriages or even suggestions of who may be eligible. Truth was, at almost 50 years old, with 'teeth few, poor and blackish; his hair was thin and white', he wasn't really a particularly appealing proposition for young ladies on the Continent. Henry's search for a new wife overshadowed some of the negotiations that were taking place for his son and his daughter and meant that the progress made on behalf of the children was painfully slow.

One other thing that may have explained this lack of progress, or even enthusiasm, could well be the presence of Catherine of Aragon in England. Originally, following the death of Arthur, the premise had been that her marriage alliance be moved to Prince Henry, so that she would still be destined to be queen of England, and the Spanish alliance would continue uninterrupted. However, Elizabeth's death threw a proverbial cat among the pigeons. On 27 June 1505, Prince Henry stood before the Bishop of Winchester and declared that his potential marriage contract, signed two years earlier with Spain which betrothed him to Princess Catherine, was null and void. While on the surface this could simply have been a diplomatic issue, it was also a possibility that the king wanted the young princess for himself.

Catherine was considered a beauty. She was intelligent, sophisticated and exotic compared to the rest of the English court. At the time of the death of the queen, Catherine was just turning 18 years of age, and had already become well acquainted with the king, his family and his country. The Spanish alliance was crucially important to English positioning in Europe and so perhaps it crossed the king's mind that he should be the one to marry Catherine rather than his 12-year-old son. Negotiations had been ongoing for Prince Henry to marry the daughter of the Duke of Angoulême, and perhaps this offered them a way to ensure that everyone was happy with arrangements going forward.

However, there seems to have been reticence, more so on the part of the Spanish. For them, though, there were more important things going on than worrying about a treaty with England. In November 1504 Queen Isabella of Castile died. She had been the monarch, with Ferdinand, her husband, as merely her consort. When she died, the crown of Castile passed to Isabella's daughter Joanna. This caused issues; Ferdinand tried to rule as her proxy, as she had married Archduke Philip, the son of Maximillian, the Holy Roman Emperor, and was therefore too far away to rule in Spain. Philip, however, argued that his wife was mad, and therefore the throne was his to rule in her stead, not her father's. This argument continued until, in January 1506, Philip himself led a fleet from Flanders to Spain, to try to take the throne by force. Unfortunately for Philip, the weather turned against him and he and the fleet were forced to land on the English coast. Some sources even refer to them being 'shipwrecked' at Melcombe Regis, which was a small village just up the coast at Weymouth. Melcombe Regis and Weymouth are both in the natural harbour created by Portland Bill, and the ships would have taken refuge in the calmer waters, but Dorset in 1506 was isolated and there was very little there for a fleet of Spanish ships, let alone Spanish royalty.[2]

Letters were sent immediately to Henry VII to let him know of their arrival, which took everyone by surprise. He invited them to Windsor, and sent litters and carts to transport them, but Queen Joanna was not able to travel, too shaken by the ordeal of being 'shipwrecked' in a foreign land. Instead she and the rest of the royal party were taken to a local house, Wolfreton Hall, near Dorchester, in order for them to rest and recuperate. While they stayed in Dorset a full welcome, led by 14-year-old Prince Henry, was arranged at Winchester, a much shorter journey from Dorset for the queen to have to endure.[3]

For King Henry this impromptu royal visit by the Spanish party was a gift. He had had no progress in furthering the alliance with Spain due to their ongoing domestic issues, but now they were on his shores and owed him for his hospitality. He was able to make the most of their presence and managed to get them to re-sign the Treaty of Medina del Campo, but the question of marriage to Catherine of Aragon was left as an open issue since her father, who ultimately was responsible for her, was still alive. Relations between Henry and Ferdinand were strained still, as he had failed to pay Catherine's dowry in full, even five years after her arrival in England. But now, Henry had the cooperation of Castile, and a connection to Maximillian I, so England's relationship with Spain and huge swathes of Europe was, for now, secure. News of the Spanish arrival even reached Scotland, and King James IV, Henry's son-in-law, wrote to Philip to praise the king and to encourage him for having 'thus been drawn into a closer alliance with King Henry'.[4]

This renewed alliance also included proposals of marriages for all of the members of the family. Philip put forward suggestions that Henry himself could marry his sister, Margaret of Savoy. Mary would be betrothed to Prince Charles of Castile, Philip's son and heir, and Prince Henry would be promised to Philip's daughter, Eleanor.[5] Of these three suggestions through, only Mary's betrothal would ever actually be accomplished.

Margaret of Savoy was not consulted and, having already been married and widowed twice, was not keen on the idea of another marriage to a man she did not know. Maximillian I was not happy about delays on either side of the proposal and in July 1506 wrote to Henry to attempt to speed up proceedings, but they never went any further.[6] In the same way, Prince Henry's betrothal to Eleanor never really took off either, most likely because the marriage of Mary to Charles took precedence and too many marriages between the same family was never really a good idea.

Philip died in the autumn of 1506, which left Henry to negotiate Mary's betrothal and marriage with Emperor Maximillian, Charles's grandfather. The emperor, while powerful, was monetarily poor, and was persuaded to let the betrothal go ahead when Henry offered him a loan of 100,000 crowns as part of the negotiations. In December 1507 a treaty was signed between the two parties and this agreed that the following Easter the betrothal ceremonies would be completed, and then marriage would take place as soon as Charles reached 14 years of age. The treaty was a reason to celebrate, not just for Henry having secured a strong alliance with the Holy Roman

Empire and the Spanish in one swift move, but also for people all over England. Trade with the Holy Roman Empire had been fraught but thanks to the treaty it opened up once more, allowing English traders with the Low Countries in particular to prosper.

With all the comings and goings, treaties and negotiations, it became increasingly confusing for all involved to know who the royal household were betrothed to, and the ever-changing circumstances meant that the children themselves were left unsure about their own fate. Mary's uncertainty was resolved when arrangements for her betrothal to Charles were eventually settled. However, Prince Henry's fate particularly remained in a sort of limbo, as did Princess Catherine's – she was unable to return to her homeland, but there was no purpose to her staying in England. Interestingly, a letter from Prince Henry in 1506, a year after he had declared their betrothal nullified, suggests he might not have given up the idea of marrying her himself, referring to her as 'my most dear and beloved consort, the princess my wife'.

The royal children were separated, some in different countries altogether. This previously close, happy family unit was now more utilitarian in nature, and their relationships became strained. The remaining siblings both prepared as best they could for the roles that they would be expected to fill, while their father remained preoccupied with ensuring that the country was stable and secure, ready to hand over to his son when he was old enough.

Prince Henry was expected to prepare for kingship just as his brother had done. His tutors adjusted his learning to ensure that he was as prepared as he could be, but to some extent, the king did not accept his younger son's abilities to rule – or to learn how to rule. The prince was not scholarly and serious as Arthur had been, instead preferring the company of other boys, and hunting, hawking and sports. He did have talents for theology and classics though, which his tutors tried to encourage, and he enjoyed the more modern, renaissance thinking coming over from the Continent in his teenage years. His humanist connections and leanings began to flourish, influenced by his tutors and the books he was exposed to.

A love of books is one thing that the king and his son had in common. When he had come to power, King Henry had created the position of royal librarian, and commissioned printers to make copies of books to go straight into the royal library. This included new editions of classic works, but also new works that were coming out of the printing houses in Europe. Henry had come to learn about this work while he was in exile and he felt it was important that the English monarchs had a royal library just like their counterparts in Europe.[7] This library would become the main source for Prince Henry in his preparations and studies after his brother's death, and while in the beginning the collection was, as Kipling describes, 'obviously without humanistic direction', the more books that entered the collection, the more these opinions came into view. The majority of the collection was in French, romances and chivalric histories, which accounts for Henry's knowledge of the Arthurian legends that were a popular part of this kind of literature. This library was also a part of the thought that '[knights] utterly ignorant of good letters rarely excel in arms', which came from John Tiptoft, a scholar who lived 1427–1470, and with whose literature Henry would have been very familiar. While it was commonly thought that too much study could make a boy weak, and that reading and scholarship could be seen as a more feminine trait, the fact that the king himself patronised books, writers and scholars throughout his reign, meant that his sons and his daughters were encouraged in their loves of the same things.[8] The royal library was at the heart of Prince Henry's preparations. He never spent time running councils as his brother had done, or was sent out to the country, probably due to the king's worries that he would become ill and then there would be no heir to his legacy or to inherit his throne. Instead, the prince remained at court and learned statecraft from his father; his mother's influence, and that of his grandmother, Lady Margaret Beaufort, encouraged the boy in his studies and preparations.

King Henry's position on the throne was still uncertain, despite nearly twenty years of concerted effort to make it secure and to build up England in the European political sphere, he still feared that yet more pretenders or challengers to his position would surface, and he worked tirelessly right up until his death to ensure a smooth succession to his only remaining son. Despite failing health, and obvious struggles with grief from the sheer amount of loss and trauma he had experienced, he still tried to put his family, and his crown, first.

In his final years Henry also focused some of his energy in ensuring that his wishes would be carried out after his death.

He kept his will up to date, covering the eventuality that his son wouldn't reach majority age before he died. His health continued to deteriorate and every winter he would suffer with more and more extreme chest infections and complaints. He also commissioned artwork, and had designs drawn up for a new tomb and chapel in Westminster Abbey where he and his wife, Queen Elizabeth, could be interred together. He bought tapestries and busts to decorate it, had poetry and histories of his reign written down for posterity, and made sure that his building projects, especially the palaces at Richmond and Greenwich, were completed. Henry's aim was to leave a legacy for his son to inherit, and pass on to all of his heirs that, he hoped, would follow after.

Chapter 11

Queen Margaret

While Prince Henry was learning to take over as king from his father, Margaret was in Scotland already fulfilling her role as Queen of Scots. When she left Collyweston in July 1503, Margaret took with her a huge retinue that would travel north through England on their way to the Scottish borders. The journey would take weeks and at each stop she would be met by huge crowds wishing her well and showing just how loved she was all over England.

Throughout the journey Margaret was accompanied by the Earl of Surrey and his men as her guard. Lady Surrey acted as Margaret's chaperone, but also took on the task of ensuring that Margaret did her duties properly, was dressed appropriately and spoke correctly. The Bishop of Moray, Scottish Ambassador to the Tudor Court, also accompanied the princess, and the Bishop of Norwich also travelled for part of the journey. There was also a huge number of various lords, knights and squires, all of whom carried banners and protected the princess while she was on the move. Margaret rode most of the way, 'rich dressed and mounted on a fair palfrey', immediately behind her standard bearer came her master of the horse, Sir Thomas Wortley, who led a spare horse and also commanded the litter that followed, just in case Margaret tired of riding.[1] Behind that her ladies and their squires rode and the older ladies who were in her party were provided with a fine carriage in which they were carried. Despite the luxurious appearance of the carriages and litters, the roads in this period were little more than rutted tracks and the journey would have uncomfortable to say the least. Behind the ladies and squires in their finery, baggage carts carrying Margaret's wardrobe, the luggage belonging to everyone in the retinue as well as provisions for the soldiers and the horses, would travel. Some of these carts would go in front of the main convoy, sent ahead to make preparations at the accommodation that they would use that night.

Whenever this parade entered a town there were also heralds who bore the royal arms on their colourful tabards, and groups of musicians and minstrels who would entertain the crowds. The soldiers who accompanied the Earl of Surrey would be deployed along the routes, to control the crowds that would show up to catch a glimpse of the princess of England and queen of Scotland.

The route Margaret took after leaving Collyweston generally headed north, but stops were planned in order for her to be able to stay in the most appropriate houses and abbeys, as well as making the biggest impression on the way. While it was important to the king that his daughter arrive safely in Scotland, the fact that she was so popular, as well as the importance of the treaty and marriage alliance with Scotland, was too good an opportunity for Henry to ignore. So the route took in major towns and cities, where Margaret would take part in civic ceremonies and represent the royal family while on her progress to Scotland; a last act as a member of the English royal family before she became Queen of Scots.

The processions stopped at Grantham, Doncaster, Tadcaster and York, and then on to Durham, Newcastle and Berwick, before crossing the border and meeting with the king of Scotland's representatives at Lamberton Kirk, just over four miles north of Berwick. At each stop, representatives would travel on to the next to ensure a safe and smooth handover, and in a lot of cases they would stay on for a considerable time. By the time the group reached the Scottish borders it is estimated there were nearly 2,000 people travelling with Margaret. That number of people arriving in such splendour in towns and cities all over the north-east of England would have been a very impressive sight, and each place tried to welcome Margaret in the most spectacular way possible.

In Lincoln, Margaret was met by Sir Richard Dymock, the Sherriff of Lincoln, who had a company of thirty horses greet her at the city gates. A choir of monks and friars sang as she entered the city and as she reached the cathedral, Margaret was given a cross to kiss by the Bishop of Norwich. All along the route similar displays were put on, from William Scargill, the Sheriff of Yorkshire, who had his horses trimmed with gold and silver bells as they lined Margaret's route, to the Earl of Northumberland who joined the procession on a horse covered in crimson velvet with gilded stirrups.[2] By this point in the journey, John Yonge, sent as chronicler, appears to have given up trying to keep track of the people joining the progress through the country as, instead of noting each individual, he simply writes that 'many other noble squires and gentlemen of Yorkshire also came to her'.[3]

At Tadcaster, Margaret was joined by Lord and Lady Latimer and even larger contingents of gentlemen, and outriders who were sent ahead to make preparations at their next stop, the ancient city of York. When the Mayor of York, Sir John Guillot, was told just how large the approaching party was, he panicked. He could see that the party would struggle to enter the city through the narrow city gates, so he ordered that a new entrance be made to the city for the party to fit through. A crude hole was made in the city walls, and later a new gate and archway constructed. This is now known as Queen Margaret's Arch, and a plaque marks the spot, telling the story of Margaret's visit while on her progress to marry the King of Scots.[4] While these are still present today, there is little evidence to show that this is in fact the place where Margaret's party would have entered the city. However, Margaret would have stayed at the bishop's palace, which is now known as King's Manor, and sits just across the square from the arch, so perhaps she would have known that part of the city, even if she did not enter it in the area.

It wasn't only Margaret's retinue that filled the streets at York. As she and her procession entered the city, the streets were filled with people, as far as the eye could see. John Yonge writes: 'all the windows were so full of nobles, ladies, gentlemen, damsels, burgesses and others in so great multitude that is was a fair sight to see.'[5]

Margaret was supposed to travel into the city and meet with the Archbishop of York at the Minster. This short journey, a distance of a quarter of a mile, took two hours as the party was slowed to a crawl by the throngs of people trying to see her and greet her. The same thing happened the next day, a Sunday, when Margaret attended church dressed in a gown of cloth of gold, a golden cape that went from her shoulders to the ground, and jewels adorning her collar and headdress. She led the procession from the front, allowing everyone to see her, providing a spectacle of beauty and strength that no one would ever forget.

After York, Margaret travelled to Durham, where she attended the installation of the new bishop, and she was greeted as his guest to all of the celebrations. She then went on to Newcastle, where children assembled at the city gates and sang hymns while she entered, and then to Alnwick, where she enjoyed a break from the travelling in the relative isolation of the castle there. By 30 July Margaret had arrived at Berwick, where the soldiers stationed at the border town fired a gun salute from the city walls as she approached.

The next day Margaret and her party crossed the border and met the Archbishop of Glasgow at Lamberton, and from that point on she was to be greeted as James's wife and the queen of Scotland, instead of Margaret Tudor, daughter of King Henry, princess of England. Her identity switched immediately, but her popularity and the throngs of people still flocked to see her as she travelled from Scottish castles and abbeys to Edinburgh to meet her future husband. When she arrived at Fast Castle, a formidable coastal fortress looking out over the North Sea, Yonge writes that over 1,000 Scots came to greet her, half of those on horseback. Although most of the lords and ladies that had accompanied Margaret left her as she crossed the border, they were replaced with Scottish lords and ladies who would accompany her on the rest of her journey.[6]

The party then travelled to Dalkeith where, a full five days before the pair were scheduled to meet for the first time, King James IV arrived unexpectedly at the castle to meet his bride. Officially he had been hunting nearby, heard of her arrival and had wanted to meet her immediately. However, he was dressed in a crimson velvet jacket, trimmed with gold, and was carrying a lyre across his back. Whatever the excuse he made for his visit, he obviously made a good impression, bowing low to Margaret and all the ladies present, and kissing their hands.[7] He stayed for the evening meal and the couple talked and appeared comfortable in each other's company and the king left to return to Edinburgh, happy with his bride, and she with him.

He returned the next day, following a tragic fire in the stables which had resulted in the deaths of Margaret's favourite horses. He came to cheer her up, ordered music and dancing, and they both played instruments and sang. The next day James returned again, and the couple again played music for one another, and sang to one another. A couple of days later Margaret received horses, a gift from James to replace the ones she had lost in the fire, and as a token of his affection just before their wedding.

As Margaret reached Edinburgh these displays of affection continued. The king met her on the edge of the city, and rode alongside her litter as they entered the city. There were displays and pageants lining the streets and people everywhere cheering and enjoying the spectacle. James commanded that Margaret's horse, one of the ones he had gifted to her, be brought and he mounted it, and hoisted Margaret into the saddle behind him. They entered the centre of the city together, at the head of the procession to the cheers of the crowds and the choirs 'singing joyously for the coming of so noble a lady'.[8] At the centre of the displays was a shield, held aloft by a unicorn and a greyhound, the Scottish heraldic animals, with a thistle and rose intertwined in the centre. These symbols recurred throughout the wedding celebrations. William Dunbar's wedding ode is another example:

Nor hold no other flower in such dainty
As the fresh rose of colour red and white
For if thou dost hurt in thine honesty
Considering that no flower is so perfite
So full of virtue pleasance and delight.[9]

On the morning of the wedding, a grand procession of ladies headed towards the chapel at Holyroodhouse, all 'richly arrayed, some in gowns of cloth of gold, the others of crimson velvet and black. Others of satin and tinsel, of damask of many colours, hoods, chains and collars upon their necks.'[10] The gentlemen in attendance all wore similarly refined dress, and all wore their chains of office to show their rank and their responsibility, either to the new queen or to their king. The Earl of Surrey wore his chains for the Order of the Garter to represent his relationship with the king of England. King James wore white damask with crimson sleeves, and Margaret matched him, her long auburn hair flowing down her back under a coif. After the reading of the papal dispensation, needed due to their close blood relationship, they exchanged vows before the archbishops of Glasgow and York, and then a short coronation ceremony followed where James himself presented Margaret with one of the sceptres of state. According to those present, throughout the ceremony James had hold of Margaret's hand or an arm around her waist.[11]

Throughout these events it is important to consider that Margaret was just a teenage girl, leaving her father, her siblings, and her familiar surroundings to enter a foreign country and marry a man she had never met. Even for someone in Margaret's shoes, who had been preparing for this for months or years, it would still have been a frightening experience, overwhelming in its scale and complexity, and she was expected to perform her duties without complaint or extremes of emotion. When she arrived in each town or city to massed crowds, or when she was expected to sing, dance or even mount a horse with a man twice her age and that she barely knew, she appears to do so with a dignity, poise and purpose that is admirable from a girl of not-quite 14. So, it is hardly surprising that following her wedding, she writes home to her father to let him know how events have gone and that she arrived safely to fulfil her duty:

> My most dear lord and father, in the most humble wise that I can, I commend me unto your grace, beseeching you of your daily blessing and that it will please you to give hearty thanks to all your servants which by your commandments have given right good attendance.

As the letter continues, the formality drops away to show just how overwhelming the whole experience was for the young Margaret, as she writes not as a princess to her king, but as a daughter to her father:

> I would I were with your grace now and many times more, when I would answer. For this that I have written to your grace, it is very true, and I pray God I may find it well for myself. No more to your grace at this time, but our Lord have you in his keeping. Witten with the hand of your humble daughter, Margaret.[12]

Maria Perry describes these last lines as a *cri de coeur* from Margaret, as a frightened young girl, homesick and realising the finality of the journey she has just taken. She did not return to England in her father's lifetime, and the thought of leaving her home and never seeing her father again, as is shown in those final lines of the letter, was obviously painful for the young girl. We do not have any letters from Margaret to her siblings in those early days of her marriage, however, the letter to her father would suggest that she would write to those she had left behind and perhaps, despite being allowed up to twenty-four

English courtiers in her household, she still would have missed the familiarity of home in England.[13]

Margaret does seem to have made the best out of her time in Scotland, and she and James went on to have six children together. Notably her first child, James, Duke of Rothesay, wasn't born until February 1507, over three years after the pair were married, and when Margaret was 17. Perhaps this was due to how busy the pair were and them being unsuccessful at conceiving a child when they were together, however, their other children were conceived and born in relatively quick succession, with gaps no bigger than a couple of years, which suggests that there was a purposeful decision to wait until Margaret was older to try to conceive an heir. Perhaps the words of her grandmother's stories of her own experience coloured Margaret's decisions and made her push for them to wait, just a little while, in the hope that risks would be reduced. The couple seemed to enjoy each other's company generally, and gave each other extravagant gifts regularly, and James – perhaps meant romantically – even named a warship after her.

However, the peace and the prosperity that had been promised by the Treaty of Perpetual Peace was not to last, and Margaret's own fate, as well as that of the Tudor dynasty would be wrapped up in the events that followed her father's death in 1509. Of the three Tudor siblings, it could be argued that Margaret was the most successful in achieving the aims of her father, and even before his death she had proved herself to be a dependable and refined Tudor princess and Stuart queen.

Chapter 12

Queen Mary

In 1503, when her sister left to start her journey to Scotland, Princess Mary was only 7 years old. She was the youngest sibling, and with her brother now preparing for kingship instead of serving as her playmate in the nursery, Mary was all on her own. She was still only a young girl, but she, in some respects, took on the role that had previously been filled first by her mother and then by elder sister, becoming more active at court occasions and becoming the centre of attention when the need called for it. She enjoyed clothes, with money being spent on her wardrobe by her father, and as part of her everyday household expenses, adding up to hundreds of pounds. She also loved music and seems to have been admired by everyone who met her. Her looks and elegance were commented upon by courtiers and ambassadors, as she was so unlike her sister, with golden hair and fair skin she resembled her mother's side of the family.

When Archduke Philip and Queen Joanna were entertained at court, Mary, alongside the Princess Catherine, were part of the welcoming committee. At the time of their visit to court she was almost 11 years old, and according to the chroniclers of the events, 'In everything, she behaved herself so well.'[1] In fact, Philip himself was so taken with her that he invited her to come to see his musicians play, all the way from the palace in central London out to Croydon. Mary was involved in all aspects of the visit, from start to finish and despite being the youngest and least experienced, she made a fantastic impression on Philip particularly. What is interesting is that Princess Catherine also featured so prominently. Queen Joanna was her elder sister and it was the first time the two had seen each other in almost a decade. Catherine would, alongside Princess Mary, help her sister to settle into the accommodations that were put aside for her, and to understand the English customs. On top of this, Prince Henry was also there, alongside Princess Catherine as the more prominent and highest-ranking dignitaries after the king, acting as the Prince of Wales, and the dowager princess, the pair were already proving quite the double act.

It was on Princess Mary that Catherine would have the biggest influence, helping her to navigate court etiquette and formal events, in the stead of her mother or any other older female family members. While Lady Margaret Beaufort was still present, her focus tended to fall on Prince Henry, as the heir to the throne, instead of his much younger sister. Catherine also enjoyed the princesses company. She was young and vivacious and enjoyed music and dancing just like other young girls. She was interested in the fashions that the Spanish ladies wore, and adopted continental styles based on what they wore, such as the gable hoods and large sleeves that would become synonymous with Catherine's image.

Catherine was still a teenager herself when Margaret left for Scotland, in the same way that Catherine had seen her own sisters leave for marriages in foreign lands. The two girls had a lot in common, and Catherine could see that Mary was intelligent and capable of learning just as she had done, in the Spanish style.

Mary's education was to take place in the same schoolrooms as her brother, under the same tutors, John Skelton and others, but there were not the same expectations of her as there were for her brother. While the concentration on languages, which we have already touched upon, was there in preparation for the foreign marriage, Mary's schooling was not really a priority in the nursery or for her tutors. However, Catherine had learned a lot while in Spain, thanks to her mother, Isabella of Castile, and now she had an opportunity to pass this knowledge on to another in a similar position.

As the historian and academic Dorothy Gardiner noted in her works on female education: 'the influences of the Italian renaissance in relation to women's education reached England most directly by way of Spain … Spanish ladies of high rank were the friends of scholars and patronesses of literature.'[2]

Princess Catherine was the epitome of one of those 'ladies of high rank' and this was a major influence on Mary later in her life. Gardiner notes how Mary 'had sufficient taste for books to carry on the study of Latin', and that she passed on this love of learning in the way she educated her children later on in her life. This again is an imitation of how Princess Catherine educated her own daughter, Mary, or perhaps Catherine took her experience of helping her sister-in-law into account when dealing with her daughter.

Catherine's influence and support would have been indispensable for Mary as she got older and, in December 1508, her betrothal to Charles of Castile was formalised. When the ambassadors for Emperor Maximillian arrived to complete the negotiation they were met by the king, the Archbishop of Canterbury and Prince Henry, sat at his father's side. There was a golden canopy above them, and every measure was taken to impress the ambassadors, from the lengthy documents, magnificently illuminated, to the dowry of 250,000 crowns for the princess. At Richmond Palace, ten days after the treaty was signed, the princess stood on top of a high stage, next to the Sieur de Berghes who stood as proxy for Charles of Castile, and spoke her vows. She stood in front of the large assembly at just 12 years old and spoke in perfect, eloquent French, impressing those who were present with both her skill with the language and her confidence.[3]

At the end of the ceremony a large ring was placed on Mary's finger, trumpets sounded and Mary was heralded as the future wife of Charles of Castile, grandson of the Emperor Maximillian, and heir to the Spanish region's throne. The cerebrations were as elaborate as the build-up had been, with jousts and feasting lasting for days, at which Mary sat next to her father as she was now the highest-ranking lady at court. Even Princess Catherine was relegated below her, which was something of a bitter blow for the once Princess of Wales, who was still unsure of her own position and fate. Following the betrothal ceremony, she wrote letters, that still survive, pleading with her father to send money, or to send her word about her possibilities for another marriage, or a return to Spain. Anything that would see her situation improved from the current purgatory that she found herself in.[4]

To make matters worse for Catherine, while she struggled to maintain her financial position at court and felt abandoned by her own family, Mary received gifts from the emperor and from Charles, her betrothed, of rubies set with diamonds, and a necklace with 'K' for 'Karolus', again set with pearls and diamonds, and inscribed with 'Mary has chosen the best part, no one shall take it from her'.

This necklace has been lost, but it is the reason behind the controversy over the woman in the portrait by Michel Sittow being identified by some historians as Mary. Others have identified the portrait as one of Catherine of Aragon, with the 'K' in the jewellery representing her own initials. However, some would say that the 'K' necklace Mary received as her gift from Charles matches the description and would have been in Mary's possession at this time also.[5,6]

The accounts of the ceremonies and celebrations of the betrothal were printed and distributed, with woodcuts showing details of the decorations and all those present at the court. These depictions and descriptions bore Henry's royal crest and showed the formalised alliance between England and the Holy Roman Empire, for the benefit of enemies or those who would challenge it. It was pure propaganda on Henry's part, but he also had it translated into Castilian Spanish and a copy sent to Princess Catherine's father, Ferdinand of Aragon, who was also Charles's grandfather. The fact that his daughter was present at the events, and was so miserable with their outcomes, must have made the descriptions even more vivid to Ferdinand and serve to remind him of his duties to his daughter. Henry definitely hoped he would remember his responsibilities soon so that the burden of the cost of Catherine's household would no longer be his.

The experiences of her sister, and other women around her, such as Catherine, must have been an ever-present shadow for a young princess Mary. She was fulfilling her duty, hosting at court alongside her father and brother, but was not in any control of her fate. However, she was being prepared to be a 'continental queen', and so she was able to assert some authority and have some influence over her own outcomes and what she wanted from life. This could have been because she was the youngest child, and the events that had surrounded her older siblings, particularly Arthur and Margaret, meant that Mary's future was somewhat overlooked. The death of her mother at a young age would also have changed her perspectives, and her experiences. Unlike her siblings, who would have had to go through their mother's household to get to their father's, Mary was always able to deal immediately with her father and perhaps this gave her more of an insight into how to deal with kings – and men generally. She was involved in diplomatic roles on behalf of her father from such a young age that dealing with people, of all ranks and nationalities, became second nature.

This confidence and ability to act calmly in the diplomatic world was a skillset that would prove incredibly valuable to her as, within months, the whole court as well as he own future would be turned upside down. When her brother Henry inherited the throne, he decided that the alliances made by his father were too cautious and set about changing the foreign policies and standing of England completely. For Mary this meant that instead of honouring the betrothal to Charles of Castile, and marrying him once he was old enough, she was now at the mercy of her brother's wishes.

By 1513 England had declared war on France, and consequently Scotland, who were allies of the French. The marriage of Mary to Charles had been delayed because the e emperor did not want to get mixed up in the diplomatic mess that England's foreign situation was becoming. In response, as part of the peace negotiations between England and France, Mary was offered up as a potential wife to the king of France, Louis XII. In July 1514, in a small ceremony overseen by Thomas Wolsey and a number of other nobles, Mary stated that she renounced her contract with Charles and that she did so freely. However, those present noted that she did not do so with her usual confidence and charm, instead making the statements short and quiet, and insisting on very little in the way of ceremony. A week later England and France were officially at peace, and Henry wrote to the Pope to request an annulment of the previous betrothal on the grounds that Maximillian had been the one to break the contract by not making the marriage happen.

Similarly, Charles himself was said to be upset by the failure of his long-anticipated marriage to Mary. He was angry at his advisors for allowing the marriage arrangements to fall apart, so they tried to appease him saying that he was only young and 'The king of France is the first king in Christendom and having no wife, it rests with him to take for his wife any woman he pleases.' According to stories told at the time, Charles brought a hawk into the council chambers and began to pluck it, saying that they had caused him equal harm, 'because I am young, you have plucked me at you good pleasure … but bear in mind for the future I shall pluck you'.[7]

Marriage arrangements proceeded quickly, and with very little input from Mary herself. She was expected to marry the much older, ailing king as it was her brother's wish. According to letters from later on, Mary had managed, probably thanks to her diplomatic experience in dealing with men like her brother, to negotiate terms that she would 'marry Lewis of France, though he was very aged and sickly on the condition that if she survived him, she should marry whom she liked'.[8]

Henry and Louis wasted no time and by September preparations were beginning for the wedding to take place in France, and Mary left England accompanied by several of her ladies, including a young Anne Boleyn. She and Louis married on 9 October 1514, when Mary was 18 years old and the king was 56 and described as 'old, feeble and pocky'.[9] Mary's motto 'To do God's will is enough for me', makes it clear she went because it was her duty; even though she was given gifts of jewels and clothes when she was received in France to make her experiences as queen more pleasant, she only went on terms that she was happy with. There was an expectation that she would produce a son for the king, but whether it was Mary who put forward her ultimatum, or Henry, or even Wolsey who tried to sweeten the deal by promising her more in return for her sacrifice, Mary left England knowing that she should, if she was lucky, be able to return soon.

Chapter 13

Long Live the King

In January 1509 Henry VII was suffering with another bout of weakness in his chest, which made him want to change his will just in case the worse was to happen. He was 53 years old, had been on the throne for almost twenty-four years. His health had been deteriorating for some time, but he had doggedly kept going, determined to see England left in the secure hands of an adult male heir, and his daughters married to allies that made England more stable and less of a target from foreign threats. With Mary's marriage betrothal the previous December, and Prince Henry now 17 years old, the king started to see that maybe, just maybe, he would be able to make his dream of a Tudor dynasty into a reality.

On 21 April 1509, Henry VII died at Richmond Palace. The throne passed seamlessly to the new king, the 17-year-old Prince Henry. While he had been preparing for this event since the death of his brother, it still must have been a shock to him, and to the entire court. While the king's health was failing, it had been doing so for several winters and so it is entirely plausible that the court would have expected the king to recover, as he had done before. He wasn't particularly old, and his style of personal rule meant that he was still very involved in everyday administration until a few days before his death.

King Henry's funeral was an extravagant affair and, owing to the old king's forward planning for his death, went ahead pretty quickly after his death. On 9 May, a little over two weeks on from his death, the king's coffin, borne on a chariot and covered in cloth of black velvet and gold, and on top his effigy holding the devices of state under a golden canopy, made its way slowly from Richmond to St Paul's Cathedral, followed by over a thousand mourners. The coffin laid in state until the morning of 10 May, when the Bishop of Rochester, John Fisher, gave an hour-long eulogy in front of the assembled mourners, which included Catherine of Aragon in her capacity as ambassador for Spain. Following the eulogy, the coffin was moved once again, this time to Westminster Abbey to be buried early in the morning on 11 May. His coffin was lowered into the crypt to lay next to that of Elizabeth of York, and above it, masses were spoken, and the staffs of office broken and thrown into the crypt. The Garter King of Arms then declared in Latin, 'The Noble King Henry VII is dead', and then, following a pause announced, 'God send the noble King Henry VIII long life'.

After the funeral was over, the construction of the Lady Chapel and the beautiful brass effigies that would lay on top, would begin immediately. Pietro Torrigiano's memorial would come to dominate the Lady Chapel, and the king's descendants and heirs would also be buried in this brand-new section of the abbey. On the front the tomb a plaque reads:

> Henry VII rests within this tomb, he who was the splendour of kings and light of the world, a wise

> and watchful monarch, a courteous lover of virtue, outstanding in beauty, vigorous and mighty; who brought peace to his kingdom, who waged very many wars, who always returned victorious from the enemy, who wedded both his daughters to kings, who was united to kings, indeed to all, by treaty, who built this holy temple, and erected this tomb for himself, his wife, and his children. He completed more than fifty-three years, and bore the royal sceptre for twenty-four. The fifteenth hundredth year of the Lord had passed, and the ninth after that was running its course, when dawned the black day, the twenty first dawn of April was shining, when this so great monarch ended his last day. No earlier ages gave thee so great a king, O England; hardly will ages to come give thee his like.[1]

The whole court stayed in mourning from the king's death until a period after the funeral, but the new King Henry had plans to make sure that his reign and his fathers were seen completely differently.

Roger Lockyer describes how 'the accession of Henry VIII, a handsome, energetic, young man, not yet eighteen, effectively closed the struggle between the rival houses for the throne'.[2] This stability was not, however, a given; some of the threats to his father were inherited by Henry VIII. Edmund de la Pole was still in the Tower and had the potential to cause problems should he start to garner support. Threats from overseas also reared their heads and the young king was not going to allow them to threaten him without repercussions.

Henry did not agree with his father's diplomatic efforts, at times seeing him as too cautious or even just outright cowardly. Henry VII had brokered peaceful alliances with virtually every major power in Europe, but his son considered England to be the lesser party in these alliances and believed that his country deserved more. England was no longer the unreliable cousin across the channel, undermined by in-fighting and civil war. The crown was rightfully Henry's, and England was powerful and prosperous; for Henry, England should be the most powerful country, not bending its knee to anyone – most especially the old enemy, France.

Henry's knowledge of history, of politics and of war, meant that he was not appreciative of his father's administrative style of rule, and instead he looked towards the military leaders in classical literature such as Roman emperors or Alexander the Great, and to his own ancestors who brought England to the top of the military tree, most impressively Henry V and his victories over the French, such as at Agincourt. Henry saw himself as cut from the same cloth, and wanted England, and himself, to have the same sort of prowess and to be equally victorious in battle.

It was not just Henry who wanted this. His father's style of rule had become increasingly unpopular, and through policies of high taxation and attainders of nobles he had gained a reputation of being something of a miser which, especially among the new generation of nobles and courtiers, made him very disliked indeed. Even Polydore Vergil mentioned this issue in his description, and he was Henry's personal historian: 'but all these virtues were obscured latterly by avarice. In a monarch indeed it may be considered the worst vice, since it is harmful to everyone.'[3]

There are a couple of things to consider here, however. Vergil was writing after Henry VII's death and hoping to obtain the support of the new King Henry, so perhaps he was taking the popular narrative in order to gain Henry's sponsorship. Also, Henry was attempting to differentiate himself completely from his father, who to some represented the old ways and the old wars between the houses.

In fact, there is little to suggest that Henry VII did align with the image presented of him in the nursery rhyme 'Sing a Song of Sixpence', with the king 'in his counting house, counting all his money'. As we have seen when describing large events, such as weddings and funerals, Henry VII would spend money in order to make sure that everything was done properly, and to give the right impression to ambassadors or to his subjects. He also spent money personally on clothes of gold, rich food, music, books and art, all for his own use and enjoyment, but this kind of frivolous spending did not fit with the image of authority that he was trying to project. Historian Stephen Gunn describes how Henry knew 'Good governance was required: effective justice, fiscal prudence, national defence, fitting royal magnificence and the promotion of the common weal.'[4]

For his son, however, this kind of 'fiscal prudence' was not the image he wanted, or even needed, to project. When he inherited the throne, the royal coffers were full, mainly due to his father's policies and diligence, but Henry VIII knew that in order to make a fresh start and move out from his father's shadow, he would need to make some changes and project a completely different image of England in all her majesty, and with him at the helm. As a headstrong 17-year-old, he saw his opportunity to put the knowledge he had gained from all his reading to make England into the powerhouse he thought it deserved to be.

From the moment Henry knew he had inherited the throne, the conversations turned to his marriage. He had seen first-hand the importance of making a good marriage and of having heirs to make his throne secure, so this became his priority, and for him there was only one choice as a bride, and that was Catherine of Aragon. It would fulfil a promise they had originally made to one another in 1503, but which had been in question ever since.

Catherine had been in his life for eight years. When she had arrived in 1501 to marry Arthur, she had received a very warm welcome from the population and remained popular in England. Her household had welcomed Henry's sister and she had been present at every large event since Arthur's death. She was a consummate courtier, had acted as ambassador to her father, and had helped Henry through some of the most difficult times in his life, including the death of his mother.

She was someone one he could depend upon, and they had become closer as his sister, Mary, had spent more and more time in Catherine's company and household. She was also very attractive and elegant, and her Spanish style of dress and behaviour was exotic. She was pious and Henry, who was devout in his own faith, could see that she was the epitome of femininity and piety by the standards of the day. She was well read, intelligent, and knowledgeable, and understood a lot Henry's interests, including classical literature, history and even sciences such as astrology.

A marriage between the two was also desirable diplomatically as it would ensure that the Treaty of Medina del Campo continued the alliances between England and Spain, which was important to Henry if he was to consider a war with France. For Catherine, the marriage would put her back in the position she felt she had been destined for, to be queen of England. When she had married Arthur and become Princess of Wales, she had known that one day she would be queen at Arthur's side. Since Arthur's death her position had been plagued by uncertainty and she had had to wait patiently for changes in her favour. Now, in 1509, at the age of 23, she was finally to fulfil what she saw as her destiny and become queen, and this time alongside a handsome, younger man whom she had watched grow up.

The wedding was quickly put together to allow them to be crowned alongside one another in the days that followed. On 22 June 1509, Catherine and Henry met at the Church of the Observant Friars, where Henry had been baptised, and were married in a private ceremony. There was a small celebration that evening, but all eyes were focused on their coronation, and the day after their wedding the couple took the traditional journey to stay in the Tower of London the night before.

This night must have been difficult for Henry. The last time he had spent any time at the Tower it had been immediately after the death of his mother six years earlier. Since then, the Tower had pretty much been abandoned as a royal palace, used only for official functions such as the tradition that the monarch stay there the night before their coronation. It would primarily be used as a prison and administrative building, and the royal apartments which had once been so opulent, would within a century lie in ruins.[5]

The following day, 24 June – midsummer's day – the pair processed through London to their coronation at Westminster Abbey. Pageants were laid on all along the route, provided by the local sheriffs and MPs of the individual areas of London, and poems were read out to the couple while they passed through. One such poem was written by Thomas More, who at this point was just starting out in his career as a lawyer and politician.

On the coronation day of Henry VIII, most glorious
and blessed king of the British Isles, and of Catherine
his most happy queen, a poetical expression of good
wishes by Thomas More of London,
IF EVER there was a day, England, if ever there was
a time for you to give thanks to those above,
this is that happy day, one to be marked with a pure

white stone and put in your calendar.
This day is the [end] of our slavery, the beginning of
our freedom, the end of sadness, the source of joy,
for this day consecrates a young man who is the
everlasting glory of our time and makes him your king–
a king who is worthy not merely to govern a single
people but singly to rule the whole world–
such a king as will wipe the tears from every eye
and put joy in the place of our long distress.
Every heart smiles to see its cares dispelled, as the day
Shines bright when clouds are scattered.
Now the people, freed, run before their king with bright
faces. Their joy is almost beyond their own
comprehension.[6]

The abbey was filled with ambassadors and nobility from all over England, and celebrations followed that lasted for days including feasts at Westminster Hall, ceremonies to inaugurate new Knights of the Bath in honour of the new king, and a progress around nearby towns to let the new couple be seen by their subjects. Everywhere they went the king and queen, especially the queen, were met with cheers and applause, the feelings shown in Thomas More's poem echoed in every community they visited.[7]

However, after such positivity, once again grief came into young Henry's life. Just hours after his coronation, his beloved grandmother Lady Margaret Beaufort took ill. The woman who had supported her son to reach the throne of England, and had then taken the young Tudors under her wing following the death of their mother, died on 29 June 1509 – the day after Henry's eighteenth birthday, and after seeing him installed as king in the full ceremony at Westminster Abbey; she was 66. According to some records, Lady Margaret became ill after eating a cygnet, presumably at the banquet that followed Henry and Catherine's coronation. She hadn't been suffering from particular ill health, but had had a hard life and at 66 was considered elderly; the death of her only child a few months earlier had taken its toll on her. The work that she, and her son and daughter-in-law, had been doing to ensure that England's throne passed to an heir peacefully, had come to its completion and her adult grandson was now on the throne with a promising future ahead.

She was buried in Westminster Abbey, next to her son and his wife in the Lady Chapel. A tomb, similar to that of Henry and Elizabeth's was commissioned and Erasmus wrote the epitaph which was inscribed onto it:

> Margaret, Countess of Richmond, mother of Henry VII, grandmother of Henry VIII, who donated funds for three monks of this abbey, a grammar school in Wimborne, a preacher in the whole of England, two lecturers in Scripture, one at Oxford, the other at Cambridge, where she also founded two colleges, one dedicated to Christ, and the other to St John, the Evangelist.[8]

The passing of Lady Margaret marked a kind of turning point in the lives of the young Tudors, especially Henry, but also for England and the Tudor period in general. She was the last remaining member of the family who had been directly involved in the Wars of the Roses, and the crowning of a new young king was symbolic of the beginning of a new and exciting era for England. Just as his father had been, however, Henry was keen to make sure that everything he did was for the good of his country and to make the crown stronger. He looked for signs to see that God was pleased with what he was doing and the decisions he was making, and certainly, in the beginning, all the signs were auspicious.

Almost immediately after their wedding and coronation, it became apparent that Catherine was pregnant. Just as Henry's mother had become pregnant with no delay and his father had seen this as a sign of God's acceptance, Henry gave thanks that he was equally blessed. However, in the January of 1510, Catherine went into early labour and she miscarried a little girl. Doctors and midwives crowded round to examine the queen, and they were adamant that she had actually only miscarried one of a pair of twins and that a baby would still be born later in the year. Catherine took them at their word and prepared for a spring birth that heartbreakingly never came. Another pregnancy quickly followed and almost a year to the day, on New Year's Day 1511, Catherine delivered a healthy baby, and this time it was boy and they named him Henry. The whole court celebrated with jousts and feasts to welcome the news that the king and queen had been blessed with a son and heir to carry on their legacy, and that their union was obviously God's will for England.

Chapter 14

Continuing the Dynasty

Following such joyous news for Henry and Catherine, it seemed as though all would be well, but this elation was short-lived when the infant Prince Henry, who had been named Duke of Cornwall, died at just 6 weeks of age. King Henry and Queen Catherine were understandably heartbroken, suffering yet more loss after already enduring so much in both of their short lives. Two further stillborn children followed before the arrival of Princess Mary in 1516, the only one of their children to survive infancy.[1] These losses would go on to colour their relationship and have dire consequences for their marriage, as well as put England's future in jeopardy. However, Henry's actions as king were greatly influenced by Catherine and for most of their marriage he greatly admired and respected her, leaving her as regent while he went to fight in France. As the auspicious signs at the beginning of their marriage began to unravel, Henry's pious, perhaps even superstitious, nature inherited from his father and grandmother would begin to cast shadows on his relationship not just with Catherine, but with everyone at the court, and even foreign powers.

The alliances that Henry VII had worked for so diligently were very quickly undermined as the young king put glory for England above all other things. First, by renewing hostilities with France – and in so doing going to war with his brother-in-law in Scotland and putting his sister in the middle of a diplomatic nightmare – demonstrates how impulsive Henry could be if there was something he thought was his duty or privilege to own. Changing his sister's marriage plans with little regard for her or the response of the other parties involved, gives us the impression that he was willing to do whatever he thought right to improve England's stature in the political sphere. Throughout his reign allegiances with France, Spain, the Holy Roman Emperor and Scotland all chopped and changed according to what he thought was best for England – and what he thought was best was not always what his advisors counselled. It is this disjointed, unpredictable and sometimes confusing style of personal rule that came to define Henry as a monarch, but throughout he maintained relationships with his siblings and continued to communicate his wishes, even if they did not always understand or support them.

Both of his sisters would bear the brunt of his indignation at the beginning of his reign. Margaret saw her husband killed on the battlefield at the Battle of Flodden in 1513, just a decade after they had been married as part of a treaty that promised Perpetual Peace with England. She was left a pregnant widow, and mother to an infant king, James V, who was just a year old when his father died at Flodden, and for whom she was regent for as long as she did not remarry. The death of her husband at the hands of troops who were fighting for her own brother must have made the situation truly horrifying for Margaret, who had not been back to England since her marriage – and now it looked like she would never return.

However, she did come back. Having remarried in 1514 to Archibald Douglas, the 6th Earl of Angus, Margaret was forced to leave her son in the care of regents in Scotland, and sought refuge at the English court to be protected by her brother, King Henry. Her position was one of in-between, loyal and devoted mother to her son who was king of Scotland, but a loving sister to her brother also.[2]

Mary's situation was also nightmarish, but she managed to navigate it. The marriage to King Louis of France, orchestrated by her brother and something she saw as her duty, was also her way forward. If she conceived a child by Louis she would forever be queen of France and have stature and power as a result of her relationship to the French royal house; if she did not conceive, she saw that she could have a freedom that a princess could never have dreamt of: to marry whoever she chose. On 1 January 1515, just three months after their wedding in Paris, Louis died and Mary was now a widow.[3] While the French, and her brother, tried to arrange another marriage for her, Mary acted on her own volition and married Charles Brandon, her brother's handsome, slightly roguish, childhood friend. Brandon had been sent as emissary to congratulate the new king of France, Francis I, on his accession to the throne and also to negotiate on Henry's behalf for his sister's return to England. However, the pair had known each other for a long time, had probably been romantically involved before Mary left for France, and even though there was opposition to the match there was nothing official that could stop them from marrying. They returned to England and announced their marriage – and Henry was furious that they had done so without permission, sending them away from court in ignominy. This was short-lived, and Charles Brandon was soon invited back and enjoyed a long career at court beside Henry. Charles and Mary were married for eighteen years, and had four children, the first of whom was born in 1516 and was named Henry, after his uncle. Unfortunately, Henry died when he was 6 years old, and their youngest child (also a son called Henry) also died aged 10 or 11 years old.[4]

More early losses also happened to Margaret who lost four children between 1508 and 1512, all born prematurely, or died in their first year.[5] Much like her brother and sister-in-law, she and her husband were trying to make their future secure with healthy male heirs, and tried throughout their marriage to conceive, but their children were all taken from them. It seems that all of the Tudor children endured more than their fair share of grief and suffering, and the loss of parents, siblings, spouses and then children all had a lasting impact on their personalities.

Henry VIII's life particularly is incredibly well documented and the subject of so much analysis. His behaviour towards Catherine of Aragon in the beginning of their marriage and his changing personality as he gets older takes on a new dimension when you look at the amount of loss, grief and uncertainty that he and all of his siblings were subjected to growing up. Henry's fixation on healthy children, particularly sons, would have a lasting impact on his style of rule and on his decisions throughout his life, but his experiences in childhood also influenced his style of parenting and the decisions he made for his children as they grew up.

For example, instead of sending his son Prince Edward out into the Midlands to govern the Marches, Henry chose to keep his son close. He gave Edward a humanist education as he too had received, and kept him nearby so as not to risk the same fate as had befallen his brother. So precious was Edward as a commodity, and as his only son and heir, that Henry used all of his experience to try to keep his child safe and yet still made sure that he was prepared and knowledgeable, able to take up the mantle when the time came.

Equally, Henry saw from his experiences with his sisters, mother and grandmother, that women were equally capable of learning, and this was incredibly important when the girl was destined to be a queen. While Catherine of Aragon undoubtedly had a great deal of influence over her daughter's education and upbringing, Henry too ensured that she was well educated and had a wealth of experience dealing with diplomats in preparation for her adult life. Later, Elizabeth was also given an education, despite the absence of her mother, Anne Boleyn, which suggests that Henry had learned from his own experiences and taken advice from the women in his life. While his later wives, particularly Katherine Parr, took their roles as stepmother very seriously and had a great deal to do with the children's households, Henry, as their father, was the one consistent influence on their childhoods and experiences.

The childhood experiences of both Mary and Margaret also influenced the way they became parents and how they treated their children. Thanks to Mary's influence and work with tutors, her daughters were both learned women. She also spent a lot of time in their family home, raising her children herself rather than them being separated from her. Her eldest daughter, Frances, would marry Henry Grey, and her daughters in turn would be highly educated with a reputation for their knowledge and piety. Frances's eldest daughter, Jane, was chosen by Edward VI as his heir; she was Lady Jane Grey – or as it should be, Queen Jane – who ruled for just thirteen days in 1553 before being deposed by Mary I.[6]

Conclusion

The Tudor children could arguably be seen as among the most influential group of siblings in British history. Their actions and those of their descendants have shaped the English and Scottish royal lines and can be traced all the way through to present day. However, they themselves were the product of parents who brought together the best parts of their own experiences and the traditions of the royal household, to ensure that their offspring were ready for renaissance monarchical life. Their children received an education that was inspired by the medieval expectations of chivalry and femininity, but was equally inclusive of new ideas, topics and techniques of humanism and intellectualism. They embraced new technologies such as the printing press, and international influences from Italy and Spain to improve on the traditions that had served previous generations so well.

Prince Henry in particular shows us that his humanist-inspired education and beliefs, brought about by his tutors and those around him from an early age, would mould him and his style as monarch and the decisions he would make throughout his reign. His religious knowledge would be crucial when his marriage to Catherine of Aragon fell apart, and their quest for a divorce would lead to England's break with Rome and the formation of the Church of England. As well as this, his knowledge of foreign affairs and classical history influenced his interactions with other countries and led to the ongoing feuds with France and Spain that would continue throughout his reign and beyond. The spectacular battles, and then the shows of power and influence displayed by Henry, such as the Field of the Cloth of Gold for example, were perhaps his own way of showing how far England had come and justifying his father's actions as king, while putting his own stamp on his rule.

Princess Mary, too, was influenced by the humanist education that she and her siblings received, and the multicultural experiences she had through her time spent with Catherine of Aragon and then later on in France, would lead her to bring up her own daughters in the same manner, which was unusual at the time outside of a royal household. As it happens, her granddaughter Lady Jane Grey did end up inheriting the throne, albeit for a matter of days, but it was the legacy left by Princess Mary that allowed this to happen, and for Jane and the other Grey sisters to be considered capable enough, as well as royal enough, to inherit the throne.

Margaret's education, preparations and abilities were put to the greatest test when she became a regent for her infant son, and though she struggled to keep that control and rule in his stead while still maintaining her own sense of identity, in the male-dominated world of a royal court it is hardly surprising that she was eventually excluded. However, her power and influence was always present, and her ability to read a room and navigate politically unstable ground, never left her. The skills of queenship she had learned at her mother's knee stayed with her forever and would always influence every action she performed.

Another aspect of their young lives that linked them, and moulded them into the adults they became, was their shared experience of grief and loss, instability and fear. From their earliest days the children would have been aware of their father's journey to the throne and, as much as they were taught that as the royal heirs they were chosen by God, they also saw their parents' struggles to maintain their position. Battles, both literal and figurative, were frequent and a constant shadow of which that Henry VII was always aware. While this in some ways was good because he was never complacent and was always working hard to bolster his position for his children to inherit a stable country, it was also traumatic to be in a constant state of flux and never quite knowing if the next catastrophe would be the end of everything. This may not have been something that the children were aware of in their earliest years, kept away from the world in their nurseries in Eltham Palace or other luxurious residences, but as they grew older, became more aware, and gained personal experience of the precarity of their position and lives, this would have been a spectre and a burden they all began to share with their father.

One such experience, which maybe linked Margaret and Henry more than the much younger Mary, was the loss of their siblings. The deaths of Princess Elizabeth and then Prince Edward, there in the nursery having survived the first months or years of infancy, was something that would have made the children much more aware of their own mortality. The unexpected loss of their older brother Arthur thrust their lives, roles and expectations into a state of turbulence. Then the loss not only of their baby sister, but also of their mother who was such a huge part of their young lives, cemented that awareness still further, and brought the same feelings into Mary's life for the first time too.

The little group of brother and sisters were dealing with these events, and the trauma associated with them, from a position of isolation and without the support that may have been available to lower-class children, or to children today. It must be noted, however, that mortality was something that was much more accepted as a part of everyday life. While it was never something that was welcomed in early modern England, the average life expectancy at the time was below 40 years of age, and infant mortality accounted for this low age.[1] However, I would urge people to realise that to experience the deaths of close family members, so close together and with such impact, would surely have made indelible marks on young and impressionable minds.

When we consider their actions as adults, the impact that these events had on each of them become even more obvious. Henry's names for his children, Edward and Elizabeth, were both names of the siblings he lost, and names of other family relations, perhaps demonstrating that their loss was still something that was present in his mind even well into his adult years. His preoccupation with protecting Prince Edward, be it from germs, threats or from outside influence, was something that his own father had done with him following his brother's death, and Henry shared this concern being left with only one, young, son and heir. This shared situation could explain his actions in dealing with Prince Edward in the way he did. His constant loss throughout his life, whether it be because of his actions or not, could go a long way to explain elements of his personality and any instability or compulsions that may be levelled against him later in life.

For Mary and Margaret adulthood proved just as hard to navigate, and in the same ways brought more loss and grief for them to endure. Although, the influence of women who had been in their lives as children and young adults can definitely be seen in the actions they took later in life, and these influences were not always negative. Both Mary and Margaret did their duty to their father and brother, to their monarch, by marrying for diplomatic reasons and fulfilling their side of the bargains that were made. They married, performed their roles admirably and to the letter, and then were widowed early in their marriages. Both sisters then married a man of their choice, and whatever the outcome of those marriages may have been, to have done so was a strong choice and a brave one, that may well have been influenced by seeing women such as their grandmother, Lady Margaret Beaufort, who married multiple times following her early widowhood, and each time managed to make personal gains.

Their mother's marriage had, luckily, seemed to be a happy one, which was something they could aspire to but, unlike many women of the time, they could also see an alternative course of action which, because of their position, they had in their power to take. The cautionary tale of Catherine of Aragon could also have influenced them as she sat and waited for the men who had authority over her to make decisions on her behalf, and while Catherine would probably have argued that she was in fact waiting for God's plan to play out, that may not have been seen as an option for women who had had to make such large sacrifices already.

However flawed these children may have been, and whatever the impact of their own experiences in childhood and adolescence was on their adult lives, their impact cannot be denied.

Henry's break with Rome reshaped religious life in England and beyond through to the present day. His children from his many marriages have fascinated historians for centuries, ruled for fifty-six years after their father died, and created what has been called a 'Golden Age' for England. Mary's children and grandchildren were involved in upheavals and political changes throughout the period and beyond. Margaret's marriage to Scottish King James IV created the family line that allowed for the unification of the crowns of England and Scotland when James VI of Scotland, Margaret's great-grandson, inherited the crown of England from Elizabeth I. It is Margaret's descendants who still sit on the throne of both England and Scotland to this day.

It is because of these siblings that the royal family, and the British Isles as they are today, can trace their foundation to the family of a Welshman, Henry Tudor, who landed on a beach in Wales with very little chance of becoming king. He married a princess, had a family and created a dynasty that would last for three generations. Some of his children have become legendary, some have been almost forgotten and some have been lost to the progress of time, but it cannot be denied that the children of Henry VII and Elizabeth of York have left a tremendous legacy.

Appendix 1

The Tudor Family Tree

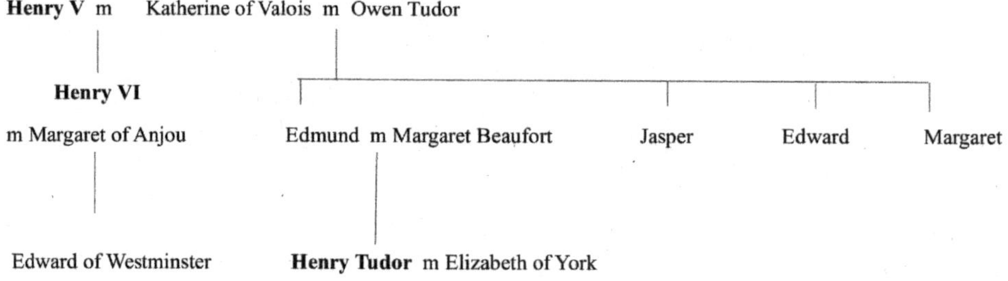

Appendix 2

The Plantagenet and York Family Tree

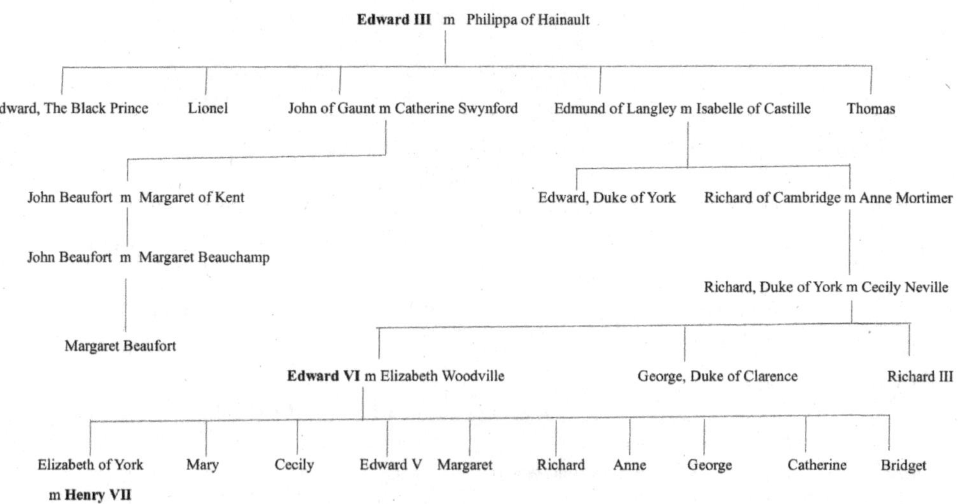

Appendix 3

The Tudor Royal Line

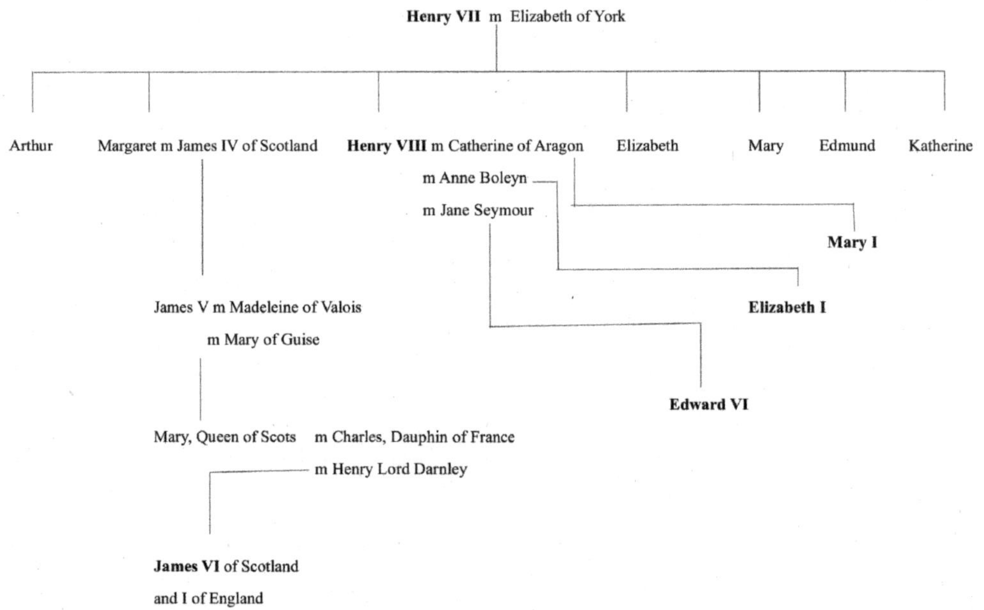

Bibliography

Primary Sources

Caius, John, *A Boke or Counseill Against the Disease Commonly Called the Sweate, or Sweatyng Sicknesse*, 1552.

Cellini, B., *Autobiography and Translation of John Addington Symonds*, Appleton, 1904.

Gairdner, James (ed.), *Letters and Papers Illustrative of the Reigns of Richard III and Henry VII: Published by the Authority of the Lords Commissioners of Her Majesty's Treasury, Under the Direction of the Master of the Rolls*, London, Longman, and Roberts, 1861.

Hall, Edward, *Hall's Chronicle: containing the history of England, during the reign of Henry the Fourth, and the succeeding monarchs, to the end of the reign of Henry the Eighth, in which are particularly described the manners and customs of those periods,* 1547, (Printed 1803)

Harris, Nicolas (ed.), *Privy Purse Expenses of Elizabeth of York [1502-3]; Wardrobe Accounts of Edward the Fourth [1480]; with a Memoir of Elizabeth of York,* London: William Pickering, 1830

Hodges, William, *An Historical Account of Ludlow Castle,* 1794.

Kipling, Gordon (ed.), *The Receyt of the Lady Kateryne*, Oxford U.P., 1990.

Mancinus, Dominicus, Armstrong, C.A.J. (ed.), *The Usurpation of Richard the Third,* Gloucester, 1984.

More, Thomas, 'A Rueful Lamentation on the Death of Queen Elizabeth' (1503), https://thomasmorestudies.org/wp-content/uploads/2020/08/Rueful_Lamentation.pdf (Accessed 12 July 2024)

More, Thomas, 'Coronation Ode of King Henry VIII' (1509), https://thomasmorestudies.org/wp-content/uploads/2020/09/Mores_1509_Coronation_Ode.pdf (Accessed 9 July 2024)

Sandford, Francis, *A genealogical history of the kings of England, and monarchs of Great Britain, &c.: from the Conquest, anno 1066, to the year 1677 : in seven parts or books containing a discourse of their several lives, marriages, and issues … with their effigies, seals, tombs … all engraven in copper plates : furnished with several remarques and annotations,* Printed by Tho. Newcomb for the author, London, 1677.

Shakespeare, William, Alexander, Peter (ed.), *The Complete Works of William Shakespeare*, Williams Glasgow: HarperCollins, 1994.

Thorpe, Lewis G.M., (translated and edited), *The History of the Kings of Britain by Geoffrey of Monmouth,* Penguin Books, 1988.

Vergil, Polydore, and Hay, Denys (ed.), *The Anglica Historia of Polydore Vergil, A.D. 1485-1537*, London, Royal Historical Society, 1950.

Tomb of Henry VII and Elizabeth of York, Westminster Abbey, https://www.westminster-abbey.org/abbey-commemorations/royals/henry-vii-and-elizabeth-of-york/

Tomb of Lady Margaret Beaufort, Westminster Abbey, https://www.westminster-abbey.org/abbey-commemorations/commemorations/margaret-beaufort-countess-of-richmond/

Secondary Sources

Amin, Nathen, *Henry VII and the Tudor Pretenders: Simnel, Warbeck, and Warwick,* Amberley Publishing, 2021.

Anglo, Sydney, 'The British History in Early Tudor Propaganda, With an Appendix of Manuscript Pedigrees of The Kings of

England, Henry VI To Henry VIII', *Bulletin of the John Rylands Library XLIV 1* (1961): pp.17-48.

Anglo, Sydney, 'Ill of the Dead. The Posthumous Reputation of Henry VII', *Renaissance Studies 1, no. 1* (1987): pp.27–47.

Anglo, Sydney, *Images of Tudor Kingship*, London, 1992.

Berry, Boyd M., 'The First English Paediatricians and Tudor Attitudes Toward Childhood', *Journal of the History of Ideas 35, no. 4* (1974): pp.561–577.

Carlson, David R., 'King Arthur and Court Poems for the Birth of Arthur Tudor in 1486', *Humanistica Lovaniensia 36* (1987): pp.147–183.

Carlson, David R., 'The Writings of Bernard André (*c*.1450 – *c*.1522)', *Renaissance Studies 12, no. 2* (1998): pp.229–250.

Carlson, David R., 'Royal Tutors in the Reign of Henry VII', *The Sixteenth Century Journal 22, no. 2* (1991): pp.253–279.

Chapman, Hester W., *The Sisters of Henry VIII: Margaret Tudor, Queen of Scotland, Mary Tudor, Queen of France and Duchess of Suffolk*, Chivers, 1974

Chisholm, Hugh, (ed.), 'Suffolk, Charles Brandon, 1st Duke of', *Encyclopædia Britannica, Vol. 26 (11th ed.)*, Cambridge University Press, 1911.

Clayton, J., Walsingham Priory in the *Catholic Encyclopedia*, New York: Robert Appleton Company, 1912, http://www.newadvent.org/cathen/15543a.htm

Clegg, Melanie, *Margaret Tudor: The Life of Henry VIII's Sister*, Pen and Sword History, 2018.

Coch, Christine, '"Mother of my Contreye": Elizabeth I and Tudor Constructions of Motherhood', *English Literary Renaissance 26, no. 3* (1996): pp.423–450.

Cunningham, Sean, *Prince Arthur: The Tudor King Who Never Was*, Amberley Publishing, 2016.

Davies, R.R., *The Age of Conquest: Wales, 1063–1415*, Oxford: Oxford University Press, 1992.

Davies, R.R., *The Revolt of Owain Glyn Dŵr*, Oxford: Oxford University Press, 1995.

Duffy, Eamon, *The Stripping of the Altars: Traditional Religion in England 1400–1580*, Yale University Press, 1992.

Gardiner, Dorothy, *English Girlhood at School: A Study of Women's Education Through Twelve Centuries,* Oxford University Press, 1929.

Griffiths, Ralph A., 'Henry Tudor: The Training of a King', *The Huntington Library Quarterly* (1986): pp.197–218.

Griffiths, R.A., Thomas, and Thomas, R.S., *The Making of the Tudor Dynasty*, New York: The History Press, 2005.

Gristwood, Sarah, *Blood Sisters: The Women Behind the Wars of the Roses*, New York: Basic Books, 2013.

Guy, John, *Tudor England*, Oxford University Press, 1988.

Guy, John, *A Daughter's Love,* London, 2009.

Hales, J.W., and Furnivall, F.J. (eds.), *Bishop Percy's Folio Manuscript, Ballads and Romances, Vol. 3*, London, 1868.

Harris, Barbara J., 'Power, Profit, and Passion: Mary Tudor, Charles Brandon, and the Arranged Marriage in Early Tudor England', *Feminist Studies 15, no. 1* (1989): pp.59–88.

Harris, Barbara J., 'Property, Power, and Personal Relations: Elite Mothers and Sons in Yorkist and Early Tudor England', *Signs: Journal of Women in Culture and Society 15, no. 3* (1990): pp.606–632.

Hay, Denys, 'The Manuscript of Polydore Vergil's "*Anglica Historia*"', *The English Historical Review 54, no. 214* (1939): pp.240–251.

Johnson, Lauren, *So Great a Prince: England in 1509*, Head of Zeus, 2016.

Kewley Draskau, Jennifer, *The Tudor Rose: Princess Mary, Henry VIII's Sister*, STA Books, 2015.

Lehman, H. Eugene, *Lives of England's Reigning and Consort Queens*, Author House, London, 2011.

Loades, D.M., *The Tudor Court*, Barnes & Noble Books, 1986

Loades, David, *Mary Rose: Tudor Princess, Queen of France, the Extraordinary Life of Henry VIII's Sister*, Amberley Publishing, 2012.

Lockyer, Roger, *Tudor and Stuart Britain 1471–1714*, London, 1965.

Lockyer, Roger, *Henry VII*, Longman, 1970.

Lytle, Guy Fitch, and Orgel, Stephen, *Patronage in the Renaissance*, Princeton University Press, 1981.

Mazzola, Elizabeth, 'Schooling Shrews and Grooming Queens in the Tudor Classroom', *Critical Survey 22, no. 1* (2010): pp.1–25.

McIntosh, Marjorie Keniston, 'Sir Anthony Cooke: Tudor Humanist, Educator, and Religious Reformer', *Proceedings of the American Philosophical Society 119, no. 3* (1975): pp.233–250.

Meyer, Allison Machlis, 'The Politics of Queenship in Francis Bacon's "The History of the Reign of King Henry VII" and John Ford's "Perkin Warbeck"', *Studies in Philology* (2014): pp.312–345.

Meyer, Allison Machlis, 'Richard III's Forelives: Rewriting Elizabeth (s) in Tudor Historiography', *Medieval & Renaissance Drama in England 26* (2013): pp.156–183.

Mitchell, Rosamund, *John Tiptoft*, London, 1938.

Monckton, Lindsav, and Steven J. Gunn, *Arthur Tudor, Prince of Wales: Life, Death & Commemoration*, Boydell Press, 2009.

Orme, Nicholas, *Tudor Children*, Yale University Press, 2023.

Orme, Nicholas, *From Childhood to Chivalry: The Education of the English Kings and Aristocracy 1066–1530*, Routledge, 2017.

Orme, Nicholas, 'The Education of Edward V,' *Historical Research: the Bulletin of the Institute of Historical Research 57, no. 136* (1984): pp.119–130.

Padel, O.J., 'The Nature of Arthur', *Cambrian Medieval Celtic Studies 27*, 1994, pp.1–31.

Penn, Thomas, *Winter King: The Dawn of Tudor England*, Penguin, 2012.

Perry, Maria, *Sisters to the King: The Remarkable True Story of Henry VIII's Sisters*, André Deutsch, 2017.

Richards, Judith M., '"To Promote a Woman to Beare Rule": Talking of Queens in Mid-Tudor England', *The Sixteenth Century Journal 28, no. 1* (1997): pp.101–121.

Ridley, Jasper Godwin, *Henry VIII*, International Publishing Corporation, 1986.

Rymer, Thomas, *Foedera, Vol. 12*, London, 1711.

Sadlack, Erin A., 'Literary Lessons in Queenship and Power: Mary Tudor Brandon and the Authority of the Ambassador-Queen', *Women and Power at the French Court, 1483-1563,* 2018, pp.117–138.

Scarisbrick, J.J., *Henry VIII*, Eyre & Spottiswoode, 1968.

Schwartz, Louis, *Milton and Maternal Mortality*, Cambridge University Press, 2009.

Sim, Alison, *The Tudor Housewife*, History Press, 2011.

Stevens, John, *Music & Poetry in the Early Tudor Court*, CUP Archive, 1961.

Streeter, Gareth, *Arthur, Prince of Wales: Henry VIII's Lost Brother*, Pen and Sword, 2023.

Unknown Author, 'The Shrine of Prince Arthur, in Worcester Cathedral, England', *The Illustrated Magazine of Art, Vol. 1, no. 4* (1853), pp.251-252

Weir, Alison, *Elizabeth of York*, Random House UK, 2014.

Weir, Alison, *Henry VIII: King & Court*, London: Vintage Books, 2008.

Weir, Alison, *Britain's Royal Families: The Complete Genealogy*, London, UK, The Bodley Head, 1999.

Whitman, Jon, 'National Icon: The Winchester Round Table and the Revelation of Authority', *Arthuriana* (2008): pp.33–65.

Endnotes

Introduction

1. Penn, Thomas, *Winter King: The Dawn of Tudor England*, Penguin, 2012, p.1.
2. 'great severity' is a quote from the Croyland Chronicle (p.504), given in the notes of Amin, Nathen, *Henry VII and the Tudor Pretenders: Simnel, Warbeck, and Warwick*, Amberley Publishing, 2021, p.30.
3. Guy, John, *Tudor England*, Oxford University Press, 1988, p.3.
4. Amin, pp.31–2
5. Family Tree for Henry Tudor and the House of Lancaster – Appendix 1
6. Griffiths, R.A., Thomas, and Thomas, R.S., *The Making of the Tudor Dynasty*, New York: The History Press, 2005. Information about the family tree of Margaret Beaufort and Edmund Tudor, their marriage and the birth of Henry VII in Chapter 1.
7. Family Tree of Elizabeth of York and the House of York – Appendix 2
8. Griffiths, Ralph A., 'Henry Tudor: The Training of a King', *The Huntington Library Quarterly* (1986): 197-218, p.05, source stated at Polydore Vergil p.03
9. Croyland Chronicles quoted in Weir, Alison, *Elizabeth of York*, Random House UK, 2014, p.122.
10. Ibid, p.123

11. Ibid, p.178
12. Ibid, p.179
13. Ibid, p.176
14. Ibid, p.178
15. Penn, *Winter King*, p.5
16. Weir, *Elizabeth of York*, p.130
17. Amin, p.37
18. Hall, Edward, *Hall's Chronicle: containing the history of England, during the reign of Henry the Fourth, and the succeeding monarchs, to the end of the reign of Henry the Eighth, in which are particularly described the manners and customs of those periods*, 1547 (Printed 1803), p.423
19. Hall's Chronicle, p.423
20. Lockyer, Roger, *Tudor and Stuart Britain 1471-1714*, London, 1965, p.9
21. Hall's Chronicle quoted in Guy, p.1
22. Hall's Chronicle, pp.424–5
23. Shakespeare, William, Alexander, Peter (ed.), *The Complete Works of William Shakespeare*, Glasgow: HarperCollins, 1994 – *Richard III*, Act 5, Scene 4, Lines 32-4
24. Guy, *Tudor England*, p.1
25. Lockyer, p.10

Chapter 1: Before the House of Tudor

1. Penn, p.6
2. Weir, *Elizabeth of York*, p.44
3. Ibid
4. Orme, Nicholas, *From Childhood to Chivalry: The Education of the English Kings and Aristocracy 1066-1530*, Routledge, 2017, p.20
5. https://www.richardiii.ca/dramatis-personae/ (Accessed 12 May 2024)

6. Weir, *Elizabeth of York*, p.60
7. Ibid, p.44
8. Ibid, p.15
9. Ibid, p.16
10. Ibid, p.17
11. Ibid, p.2
12. Ibid, p.39
13. Orme, Nicholas, 'The Education of Edward V', *Historical Research: the Bulletin of the Institute of Historical Research 57, no. 136* (1984): 119–30
14. Weir, *Elizabeth of York*, p.56
15. Ibid

Chapter 2: Prince Arthur

1. Weir, p.181
2. Hall's Chronicle, p.425
3. Sim, Alison, *The Tudor Housewife*, History Press, 2011, p.17
4. Weir, *Elizabeth of York*, p.24
5. Ibid, p.23
6. Carlson, David, 'King Arthur and Court Poems for the Birth of Arthur Tudor in 1486', *Humanistica Lovaniensia 36* (1987): 147–183, p.153
7. Picture of the Winchester round table Image 3
8. Whitman, Jon, 'National Icon: The Winchester Round Table and the Revelation of Authority', *Arthuriana* (2008): 33-65
9. Carlson, 'King Arthur and Court Poems for the Birth of Arthur Tudor in 1486'
10. Davies, R.R., *The Age of Conquest: Wales, 1063–1415*, Oxford: Oxford University Press, 1992, p.49
11. Thorpe, Lewis G.M., (translated and edited), *The History of the Kings of Britain by Geoffrey of Monmouth*, Penguin Books, 1988, p.65

12. Ibid
13. Ibid, p.71
14. Ibid, p.72
15. Ibid
16. Ibid, p.72 – see footnote relating who had entered through Totnes. It is actually amazing how many people through history, according to Geoffrey, came to Britain through the (nine miles inland!) town of Totnes.
17. Ibid, p.171
18. Padel, O.J., 'The Nature of Arthur', *Cambrian Medieval Celtic Studies 27*, 1994, pp.1–31, p.10
19. Thorpe, Geoffrey of Monmouth, p.61
20. Penn, p.2
21. Thorpe, Geoffrey of Monmouth, p.17
22. Davies, R.R., *The Revolt of Owain Glyn Dŵr*, Oxford: Oxford University Press, 1995
23. Cunningham, Sean, *Prince Arthur: The Tudor King Who Never Was*, Amberley Publishing, 2016, p.4
24. Stevens, John, *Music & Poetry in the Early Tudor Court*, CUP Archive, 1961, p.364-5.
25. Cunningham, *Prince Arthur*, p.7
26. Guy, *Tudor England*, pp.74–5
27. Gunn, Steven, and Monckton, Linda, *Arthur Tudor, Prince of Wales: Life, Death and Commemoration*, Boydell Press, 2009, p.10
28. Weir, Alison, *Henry VIII: King & Court*, London: Vintage Books, 2008, p.113

Chapter 3: Margaret, Henry, and Elizabeth

1. Clegg, Melanie, *Margaret Tudor: The Life of Henry VIII's Sister*, Pen and Sword History, 2018, p.6
2. Perry, Maria, *Sisters to the King: The Remarkable True Story of Henry VIII's Sisters*, André Deutsch, 2017, p.6

3. Scarisbrick, J.J., *Henry VIII*, Eyre & Spottiswoode, 1968, p.3
4. Anglo, Sydney, *Images of Tudor Kingship*, London, 1992, p.91
5. Anglo, *Images*, p.93
6. Ibid, p.92
7. Ibid, p.93
8. Scarisbrick, p.3
9. Harris, Nicolas (ed.), *Privy Purse Expenses of Elizabeth of York [1502-3]; Wardrobe Accounts of Edward the Fourth [1480]; with a Memoir of Elizabeth of York*, London: William Pickering, 1830, p.8, entry from 3 July 1502

Chapter 4: The Royal Nursery

1. Sim, p.7
2. Guy, John, *A Daughter's Love*, London, 2009, p.15
3. https://www.tudorsociety.com/henry-viiis-lost-sister-elizabeth-tudor
4. https://www.tudorsociety.com/henry-viiis-lost-sister-elizabeth-tudor
5. Sim, p.7
6. Ibid
7. Berry, Boyd M., 'The First English Paediatricians and Tudor Attitudes Toward Childhood', *Journal of the History of Ideas 35, no. 4*, 1974, p.563
8. Ibid, p.564
9. Perry, p.60
10. Privy Purse, p.35 onwards
11. Privy Purse, p.70
12. Ibid
13. https://www.tudorsociety.com/henry-viiis-lost-sister-elizabeth-tudor
14. Gairdner, James (ed.), *Letters and Papers Illustrative of the Reigns of Richard III and Henry VII: Published by the Authority of*

the Lords Commissioners of Her Majesty's Treasury, Under the Direction of the Master of the Rolls, London, Longman, and Roberts, 1861

15. Guy, *Tudor England,* p.70
16. Duffy, Eamon, *The Stripping of the Altars: Traditional Religion in England 1400–1580*, Yale University Press, 1992, pp.164-165
17. Sim, p.31
18. Ibid
19. Perry, p.12

Chapter 5: Education and Preparation

1. Orme, *Childhood to Chivalry*, pp.17–18
2. Perry, p.48
3. Orme, *Childhood to Chivalry*, p.182
4. Carlson, David R., 'The Writings of Bernard André (*c.* 1450–*c.* 1522)', *Renaissance Studies 12, no. 2* (1998): 229–250
5. Orme, *Childhood to Chivalry*, p.155
6. Carlson, David R., 'Royal Tutors in the Reign of Henry VII', *The Sixteenth Century Journal 22, no. 2* (1991): 253–279
7. Orme, *Childhood to Chivalry*, p.155
8. http://www.tudorplace.com.ar/Bios/ArthurPlantagenet(1VLisle).htm
9. https://thehistoryofengland.co.uk/resource/mountjoy-henry-viiis-humanist-mentor/
10. Hales, J.W., and Furnivall, F.J., (eds.), *Bishop Percy's Folio Manuscript, Ballads and Romances, Vol. 3*, London, 1868, p.258
11. Chisholm, Hugh, (ed.), 'Suffolk, Charles Brandon, 1st Duke of', *Encyclopædia Britannica, Vol. 26 (11th ed.)*, Cambridge University Press, 1911, pp.25–6
12. Perry, p.57

Chapter 6: Tragedy and Joy

1. Information about Elizabeth from Westminster Abbey website – https://www.westminster-abbey.org/abbey-commemorations/royals/elizabeth-daughter-of-henry-vii
2. https://www.tudorsociety.com/henry-viiis-lost-sister-elizabeth-tudor
3. *A historical description of Westminster Abbey: its monuments and curiosities* by Westminster Abbey 1853, p.5
4. https://www.westminster-abbey.org/abbey-commemorations/royals/elizabeth-daughter-of-henry-vii
5. https://www.westminster-abbey.org/abbey-commemorations/royals/elizabeth-daughter-of-henry-vii
6. Guy, *Tudor England*, pp.57–8
7. Clayton, J., Walsingham Priory, In The Catholic Encyclopedia, New York: Robert Appleton Company, 1912, http://www.newadvent.org/cathen/15543a.htm
8. Privy Purse, March 1502, p.2
9. Perry, p.57
10. Ibid, p.58
11. Weir, Alison, *Britain's Royal Families: The Complete Genealogy*, London, UK, The Bodley Head, 1999, p.152
12. Sandford, Francis, *A genealogical history of the kings of England, and monarchs of Great Britain: from the Conquest, anno 1066, to the year 1677: in seven parts or books containing a discourse of their several lives, marriages, and issues … with their effigies, seals, tombs … all engraven in copper plates : furnished with several remarques and annotations. Printed by Tho. Newcomb for the author*, London, 1677
13. Gristwood, Sarah, *Blood Sisters: The Women Behind the Wars of the Roses*, New York: Basic Books, 2013, p.42

Chapter 7: The Children at Court

1. Cunningham, *Prince Arthur*, p.105
2. Perry, p.57
3. Ibid, p.60
4. Ibid, p.55
5. Letters and Papers, Vol. 2, June 1502, p.340
6. Letters and Papers, Vol. 1, p.100
7. Cunningham, *Prince Arthur*, p.124
8. Letters and Papers, Vol. 1, p.103
9. Cunningham, *Prince Arthur*, p.127
10. Gardiner, Dorothy, *English Girlhood at School: A Study of Women's Education Through Twelve Centuries*, Oxford University Press, 1929, p.154
11. Cunningham, *Prince Arthur*, p.129
12. Letters and Papers, Vol. 2, p.128
13. Cunningham, *Prince Arthur*, p.130
14. Ibid, p.142
15. Perry, p.18
16. Ibid, p.33
17. Cunningham, *Prince Arthur*, p.149
18. Perry, p.62
19. Ibid, p.34

Chapter 8: The Death of Arthur, Prince of Wales

1. Hodges, William, *An Historical Account of Ludlow Castle*, 1794, p.25
2. Caius, John, *A Boke or Counseill Against the Disease Commonly Called the Sweate, or Sweatyng Sicknesse*, 1552
3. Cunningham, *Prince Arthur*, p.176
4. Ibid, p.168
5. *Ludlow Castle*, pp.5-26
6. Cunningham, *Prince Arthur*, p.181

7. Kipling, Gordon (ed.), *The Receyt of the Lady Kateryne*, Oxford U.P., 1990, p.xiii
8. Vergil, Polydore, and Hay, Denys (ed.), *The Anglica Historia of Polydore Vergil, A.D. 1485-1537,* London, Royal Historical Society, 1950, p.121
9. Perry, p.36
10. Ibid, pp.38-39
11. Privy Purse, 14 September, p.48
12. Cellini, B, *Autobiography, trans John Addington Symonds,* New York, Appleton, 1904, pp.18-19

Chapter 9: The Death of a Queen

1. Privy Purse, pp.58–9
2. Schwartz, Louis Milton and Maternal Mortality, Cambridge University Press, 2009, p.30
3. Privy Purse, pp.55, 82–3
4. Weir, *Elizabeth of York*, p.403
5. Ibid, p.404
6. Ibid
7. Ibid, p.406
8. https://thomasmorestudies.org/wp-content/uploads/2020/08/Rueful_Lamentation.pdf
9. Image of a Passional, showing Henry VII at the time of the death of Elizabeth of York, and their surviving children. Please see the pictures section.
10. Weir, *Elizabeth of York,* pp.411–15
11. Privy Purse, p.55
12. Perry, p.44

Chapter 10: The Later Reign of Henry VII

1. Lockyer, Roger, Henry VII, Longman, 1970, p.84
2. Perry, p.66

3. Chapman, Hester W., *The Sisters of Henry VIII: Margaret Tudor, Queen of Scotland, Mary Tudor, Queen of France and Duchess of Suffolk*, Chivers, 1974, Chapter 1
4. Letters and Papers, Vol. 2, p.11, Originally in Latin
5. Perry, p.69
6. Letters and Papers, Vol. 2, p.153
7. *The Receyt of the Lady Kateryne*, p.121
8. Rosamund Mitchell, *John Tiptoft*, London, 1938, p.100

Chapter 11: Queen Margaret

1. Perry, pp.45-46
2. Ibid, p.47
3. Ibid
4. Images of Queen Margaret's arch. Please see the pictures section.
5. Perry, p.48
6. Ibid, p.49
7. Ibid, p.50
8. Perry, p.51
9. Perry, p.51
10. Perry, p.52
11. Perry, p.52
12. Perry, pp.53–4
13. Rymer, Thomas, *Foedera, Vol. 12* London, 1711, p.789

Chapter 12: Queen Mary

1. Perry, p.67
2. Gardiner, pp.151–52
3. Perry, p.70
4. Ibid
5. The Sittow Portrait can be seen at the Kunsthistorisches Museum, Vienna.It is also pictured as the front cover image of Alsion Plowden's 'Tudor Women' and can be seen online.

6. https://www.theanneboleynfiles.com/katherine-aragon-mary-tudor-the-re-identification-michel-sittows-portrait-young-woman-nasim-tadghighi/
7. Perry, pp.124–5
8. Perry, p.128
9. Brown, Mary Croom, 1911, *Mary Tudor: Queen of France*, London: Methuen Publishing, p.101

Chapter 13: Long Live the King

1. https://www.westminster-abbey.org/abbey-commemorations/royals/henry-vii-and-elizabeth-of-york/
2. Lockyer, *Tudor and Stuart Britain*, p.16
3. Lockyer, Henry VII, p.84
4. Gunn, p.10
5. Weir, *Elizabeth of York*, p.405
6. https://thomasmorestudies.org/wp-content/uploads/2020/09/Mores_1509_Coronation_Ode.pdf
7. Lehman, H. Eugene, *Lives of England's Reigning and Consort Queens*, Author House, London, 2011, p.85
8. https://www.westminster-abbey.org/abbey-commemorations/commemorations/margaret-beaufort-countess-of-richmond/

Chapter 14: Continuing the Dynasty

1. Scarisbrick, p.150
2. Chapman, pp.72–4
3. Brown, pp.156-7
4. Chapman, p.13
5. Ibid, p.71
6. Guy, *Tudor England*, pp.226–29

Conclusion

1. https://ourworldindata.org/life-expectancy

Index